ORCHESTRATING LIFE-WORK HARMONY

A Life-First Model for Courageous Living

By **Trina Celeste**
CEO RizeNext Corp™
Co-Founder of Tech-Moms.org

ISBN 978-1-961716-00-1 (ebook)
ISBN 978-1-961716-01-8 (paperback)

Published by RizeNext™
rizenext.com

Edited by Lil Barcaski, GWN Publishing
Edited by Jenie Skoy
Proofread by Linda Hinkle
Cover design by Kristina Conatser
Interior design by Kristina Rodriguez
Front Cover and Author Photo by Dani Corbett-Tebbs, Lake City Photos

trinaceleste.com

Contents

Dedication

To My Boys,

Life's transformation,
Gardens bloom with vibrant hues,
Orchestrating growth.

...Okay, fine, just remember the goats.

- Love Mom

Introduction to Life-Work Harmony

Pull off the Goatsh*t! Bandage of "Work-Life Balance" and tune into "Life-Work Harmony."

–TRINA CELESTE

I remember a time in my life when the idea of maintaining a work-life balance was my number one goal. I used this mantra to keep all the balls madly spinning. As a working mother for the last twenty years, I have had too much to do, but I insisted I could get it done. I dug deep, like an explorer of lost treasure, seeking to discover that moment when my work and home life would finally balance. But that elusive moment where alignment and peace reigned never came. And what's more, I felt doomed never to get it together, yet I persisted in my efforts to succeed in this one-woman circus act called work-life balance.

I was a tightrope walker, juggler, and maniacal monkey all at the same time, clapping my cymbals to keep my life and work perfectly balanced. But that all changed in one terrible moment. All that came crashing down. Let me take you back to the weeks in my life when none of that mattered, where the only thing that actually mattered was making sure my son was alive and well.

I woke in a panic at five a.m., rushing downstairs to check on my 17-year-old son to make sure he was still alive. I knocked on the door a little too urgently. His voice came back muffled. "I'm okay, Mom," he said in a tone I knew so well. A few weeks before, I had stepped into the emergency room, relieved to find him still alive, his body outlined under a thin blanket. I rejoiced at his exhalations, the same breath that felt warm against my cheek as I held him as an infant, his white-blonde hair shining from his earliest moments. His body was curled up in a fetal position as he lay in the hospital bed, and he looked up at me blankly. When I went to touch him, he curled tighter and faced away, and his eyes closed, not ready to talk. I'll never forget what the doctor said: "He's been planning on taking his life. He's been saving his medication for months."

The doctor's words still haunt me. The pain my son must have been feeling knocked the wind out of me. I felt my knees buckling, so I took short breaths to keep from passing out on the floor. The questions loomed: Why? What caused this? Was it something I did? Had something happened at school? But in that moment, I was grateful he was safe.

My balancing act no longer mattered when confronted with this terrible realization. The scales had tipped, and all fell by the wayside, and I learned something else I didn't expect: I learned harmony.

This event taught me to put down the balls in this impossible juggling act and to take stock. We all have the same twenty-four hours in life to work with. Time is a constant, and for that reason, we are often glued to our schedules and clocks, trying to make it to the next appointment or deadline. Because the show must go on, or must it? It is what we are taught. It is drilled into us. But why are some of us zipping along while others barely hang on by a thread?

For me, maintaining a work-life balance has always felt like a precarious place to stand, where at any moment, everything could tumble down around me. The idea of balance leaves you feeling like a tightrope walker, constantly afraid of falling into some awful abyss. Even the very phrase: *work-life balance*, though touted as a positive mantra in the past, felt like a curse in the moments when my son's life hung in the balance and work demands continued to pile up.

So, maybe the question we should ask is: Why are we still working under an outdated and frankly dangerous myth called "work-life balance?"

What if you stopped trying to balance for a moment? Consider your boundaries, who or what might be sapping your energy? What if you paused to examined within, starting where every lasting change requires you to go? Are you able to tune in and hear beyond the external noise? Listen to the undercurrent of music playing, and allow it to lead you peacefully along. Take time to tune in and find harmony amid tumult and change.

What if your child's soccer game took precedence over that work report? Or what if, *gasp!* sometimes work comes first, even though people shame you for it? Can you let go?

Harmony wants you to let go of being perfect. Tune in and listen. Recognize that the math of a work-life balance, when calculated, doesn't ever add up. That's because living is not a science, it's an art, and that's why I want to introduce you to the concept of Life-Work Harmony, a concept that will help you put your life and priorities first.

Sometimes it takes cataclysmic events, like a child's call for help or a partner's addiction, to force us into new patterns. And that is how it was for me, it forced me to throw away the old pattern of balancing and instead practice tuning in and listening for harmony. I learned so much in the hospital that day and want to share it. Through trial and error, I've come to realize that maintaining a work-life balance is bullshit. Better yet, balance is goatsh*t! and you will discover why this term more appropriately serves in explaining these false ideas through the coming pages.

I have always been a hard worker, growing up on a small family farm with a milking cow, chickens, turkeys, an amazing half-acre garden, and pesky, ornery goats. As a farm kid, I knew that no matter how hard I worked, there were never enough hours in the day to get everything done. We have been spoon-fed bullshit platitudes like: "Just find balance," "You'll feel better once you create some balance!" and "You're just out of balance!" All these messages come through social influences, media, work, and from our families.

I have spent the last twenty years preaching the myth of a work-life balance, primarily to working mothers and colleagues in the technology industry. But I am here to tell you that finding the holy grail of work-life balance is impossible. It is an unrealistic ideal that buries you deeper in a growing list of never-ending to-dos and leaves you tailspinning.

I grew up with nine brothers and sisters, and we all learned the value of work. I still remember my mother's morning chore list sitting next to our breakfast cereal, a steaming bowl of cracked wheat. That list was always present, staring back at us at the beginning of the day, assignments for each of us ten kids, and the expectation that all chores would be done.

These lists were short, simple, and increased in effort with age. Mom didn't micromanage. Instead, she trusted that each of us would accept our role and responsibility. It was her way of organizing the chaos of a large family, and no one was exempt from contributing. I found fulfillment in the work. I have found continued happiness, stability, and engagement in my career, and now I impart this opportunity to integrate work with all aspects of your life.

I have seen how the message of placing your life first, then finding harmony with work, has taken hold and is changing the lives of hundreds of people. There is harmony to be found in the trombone slide of scheduling another appointment with the oncologist, the staccato piccolo of text reminders to call your accountant, and the clash of a cymbal that tells you to drop everything and talk to your teenage daughter. There is a rhythm, and there can be harmony to it, unless we are laboring under an unrealistic perception of maintaining work-life balance, leading you to a cacophony rather than a symphony.

CHAPTER 1

Balance is Goatsh*t!

"Attempting to balance work and life is like using a bandage to fix a serious wound. Rip off the Balance Bandage and open your mind to a new way of living and working."

–TRINA CELESTE

In 2019, I co-founded a non-profit for women, specifically mothers, transitioning from their current careers or re-entering the workforce. Over the last few years, these colleagues and recruits have become alumni of a growing community known as *Tech-Moms*, women eager for change in their lives, who are creating more fulfilled versions of themselves through personal and career development. They are seeking new, flexible, and more harmonious careers that accept their roles as mothers. I join at the helm of each class launch to show recruits how to find harmony between all areas in their life – but I'm quick to point out this doesn't come through "balancing."

My thirty-year career in technology "sparked" when I fell in love with programming. I took my first Pascal programming class in 1994 and immediately switched my degree from architectural engineering to computer science. I have never looked back. I learned these lessons the hard way, but I hope to pave the way for other women who struggle with this concept so erroneously taught to us.

Tuning in and listening to a small spark of interest was critical as it grew into a flame and is now an expanding inferno: a rewarding and long-standing career, working for years in roles such as a network engineer at Novell, a technical consultant at Oracle, in senior leadership roles in technology operations at eBay, the founder of a consulting firm, and now enabling hundreds of women to flame their inner spark. All these life stages have given me a set of sought-after skills and supported me during some of my life's most colossal challenges.

On the first day of coursework, we begin working with students, introducing new ideas for managing life and work to ensure their successful course completion. Every class starts with nervous energy, mixed emotions felt by women ages twenty to over seventy, non-parents, moms and grandmas, single and married, all beginning their own life-transformation journey.

Some have been out of the workforce, and others are actively working. Wherever they are starting from, they all share a common goal and a sense of hope, fear, and excitement as they strive to change the trajectory of their lives and the lives of their families. This community has since become a force of change long overdue in a culture where women traditionally stay home to raise children.

Over the years, as we have transitioned hundreds of careers, we have begun to see a commonality in the need for technical skills and the necessary life management skills which lead to successful outcomes. We are not merely doing career transitions but conducting complete life transformations. This process requires self-discovery and centering; individuals work through the challenges of their own personal 'balancing act,' requiring them to consider what kept them from achieving personal growth.

In keeping with this new tradition of bringing harmony into your life, like a musician, you start by first tuning your instrument.

In this case, your instrument is yourself, so you learn to tune in to yourself to feel and act in harmony with the outside world.

Considering that you are like an instrument, to play well, you must continually take time to tune in. Throughout this book, you will stop and "tune in." Acknowledging your thoughts, reflecting on them, and setting new goals and priorities for you to achieve harmony. Let's take a moment to tune in now.

TUNING INTO HARMONY

What thoughts have come to mind as you reflect on moving from a life of "balance" to "harmony?"

Do you feel that you are in harmony? Why, or why not?

RIPPING OFF THE BALANCE BANDAGE

As we kick off courses with our eager students, I ask them to tune in briefly to their emotions by sharing how they felt at that moment. They reply with: stressed, overwhelmed, and frustrated. They question themselves, and some even wonder why they are even there.

I reminded them that they had the courage to listen to that voice inside that said: "There is more for you. There is more in you." Some had to ignore friends, family, or colleagues who shunned their want and need for personal growth.

Many were told, "You should stay where you are."

"Why try? It will be too hard." or

"This industry is not welcoming to women. You shouldn't waste your time."

I always start classes by ripping off what I call the *Balance Bandage*. (If that phrase isn't trademarked, I'm claiming it now.) I write a single word in all caps at the top of the whiteboard. BALANCE. I am speaking from the heart because, like these women, I have been through the mill of trying to balance a busy job while being a mom. I have navigated similar unexpected life events. For me, it was illness, cancer, family mental health challenges, financial struggles, marriage, having kids, and subsequent divorce. All while working full-time, overseeing my ex-husband's company accounting, managing eight rental properties, developing my career, and attempting to keep my kids fed and happy. While my experiences are somewhat extreme, they have given me a perspective to understand the hills and valleys of life and an ability to relate to the journeys of the women I engage with.

I reinforce their courage in following their inner spark, "You have done the hardest part of this course; you showed up."

I circle the word BALANCE and, in one stroke, draw a massive X with a red dry-erase marker over the word, moving my arm wide for effect. This is how I rip off the *Balance Bandage* and open their minds to a new way of living, working, and understanding that balancing work and life is like using a bandage to fix a serious wound. I sense their minds racing, "How am I going to then manage it all?"

I have had similar thoughts so many times. The questions are loud, sometimes deafening.

How can I find time for my family? How can I continue to have a fulfilling career? When do I find time for myself? How do I ensure everyone is safe, provided for, and, in the mix of all this, still find enjoyment?

The reality of my son's struggles with suicidal ideation did not stop while my cellphone screamed back at me with triple-booked appointments popping into my calendar that day, years ago. Six months prior to his terrifying hospital visit, I had left my position overseeing technology operations at eBay to take a senior director position at Oracle, making the leap into leading a consulting organization simultaneous to COVID-19 disrupting the planet. I was building out our strategic accounts teams in a chaotic pandemic landscape. At the same time, my parents were housed in the ICU at two separate hospitals for over a month, fighting the coronavirus and for their lives.

Taking a new high-pressure position amid a global pandemic, isolating in a home office, my parents battling for their lives, and my son's suicide ideation all converging in one season brought stress and panic as I worked through how to manage each area. There was definitely no sense of "balance."

My team was fully decentralized and dispersed throughout North America and Canada, which was a fortunate benefit of already working in the tech industry. Everyone was familiar with actively working remotely in distributed teams. No one was at the same location, and we only knew each other via virtual calls, texts, emails, and, if lucky, a direct call, which usually meant something had to be handled quickly.

As if this were not enough, we had just transitioned to homeschool, and my twelve-year-old and I sat down to discover the new world of online learning. A sketch by comedian Jim Gaffigan comes to mind about some serious superintendent's decision to put our children on the same machines they play Roblox and Minecraft on, then telling them to do schoolwork and stay on task. I can see my children defending their off-task behaviors by saying: "But mom, we're great at multitasking."

My son and I reviewed how we would now connect to school virtually, and I saw his eyes gloss over behind his black-framed glasses as he began to cry. So, I called for a break and spent the afternoon kicking soccer balls in the front yard avoiding all the demands happening at that moment. After lunch, I went full swing back to work, conducting contract reviews with legal, new hire interviews as we scaled the department, engaging with my team, and client meetings.

I share these stories with the room of students attempting to balance. Often I will pause, focusing my attention on the women in front of me. I watch as they inhale and then exhale and let go of the stress of attempted balance. As they internalized removing the notion that we "need to do it all," the tension dissipates slowly, but anxious smiles will look back at me, and so I remind them: "You are all parents. You have lives, work, meetings, laundry, sports, hobbies, friends, doctors' appointments, and deadlines. You have family expectations and responsibilities. You are all juggling while walking a tightrope attempting to handle all thrown your way. You have been told you need to find balance, and I am here to tell you that balance does not exist. Balance is goatsh*t!"

And then I introduce them to harmony.

When harmony flows into our lives, even in brief stints, it gives us momentum. It fuels us, allowing us to achieve personal goals, build and maintain close relationships, and participate in purpose-filled activities like social causes. It gives us resonance as we meditate and refocus, shifting our frequency to the ups and downs that allow us to proceed and succeed.

That harmony frequency is like a consistent low buzz, like bees building a hive. The subtle sound of the hive as the bees are in a state of flow going about their work.

What if I told you that the key to harmony is simply understanding yourself and your boundaries and protecting your priorities? Setting your fence lines will protect you from getting pulled into disharmony. The requisite guard rails ensure that you *put yourself and your precious life first*, allowing harmony to flow into your life.

A centered life, and personal safety, leads to anticipated energy, joy, and excitement in your future. Throughout this book, you will spend time reviewing and reaffirming your vision and boundaries, enabling you to become stronger and more confident in your decisions and actions.

No one else can provide a harmony list tailored to your needs. There is no such idea as, "Make this list, and after you accomplish all, you will find harmony." I wish I could fly everyone to a tropical island in the middle of the Caribbean and allow you to take a month to reflect. However, this respite would only be temporary. I could send you a plate of my grandmother's cookies or sing you a song that may bring you bliss, but this would be my version of harmony, not yours.

What I can do is teach you how to identify things that bring wonderful moments of happiness and joy. Many of the methods I will share were learned through struggle. I did it the wrong way for years, seeing my life's expectations burning down around me while I ran around trying to resuscitate a sense of harmony. What I am sharing is as important to me as the lesson taught by the phoenix, and centering yourself on yourself will help you rise out of the ashes of life's biggest challenges.

Take a moment to pause and think about what tranquility would feel like for you.

TUNING INTO TRANQUILITY

What is it that makes you whir with purpose?

What makes you feel a sense of well-being that all is right in the world?

What brings you joy? Is it a place you go to? Is it a song you put on repeat? Is it a food you eat or a mantra you state?

AN ILLUSTRATION OF GOATSH*T! BALANCING ACTS

Some of our students are escaping poverty and domestic violence. I recall a phone call with one woman who spoke boldly as we discussed her dreams of finding a new career, but then she abruptly shifted to a hushed whisper, asking me to hold on. I could hear doors shutting, then rustling as she returned moments later, whispering nervously, "I'm in an abusive relationship. My husband cannot know I am taking this course. This is my path to independence."

I remember wanting to yell, "Run! Get out now!" as I envisioned her cowering and hiding in a darkened room. I asked if she was safe, and she said yes, and we took a shared deep breath and continued our conversation in a hushed whisper, creating the beginning of sparks toward gaining control of her life and the confidence to move out of harm's way. I know a little of what she feels, having escaped an addict ex-husband who never harmed me physically, though his betrayals did, deeply so.

During the pregnancy of my third son, I ignored the disruptive thoughts that his father was unwell. I was the proverbial "good wife," always taking care of things. He always had an answer, and I became accustomed to accepting his excuses. The changes were so incremental. I was so stretched thin; I didn't see the disappearing money, the randomness of his moods, and his unavailability. My work schedule was full, handling real estate at night, along with spending time with my baby and my boys. My days were so full of family and work it left zero room for me to take a deeper look.

I had attempted to balance external expectations and the demands of my work and family until it all came crashing down. I held onto the belief my church leaders and family instilled about being a "good wife" and always supportive. Leaving was deemed a selfish act, so I gave until I had nothing left to give.

I was preparing to take my son to his seventh birthday party with five of his young gentlemen friends in tow. I sat with my five-year-old and six-month-old baby, waiting in the living room for my husband's arrival. He came through quickly, waving hello, not making eye contact, then ran down the hall and ducked into the master bath. A single moment of awareness sparked my hunger for freedom from being attached to his chaos.

I tentatively walked down the hallway into the bedroom to find a locked bathroom door. I began folding laundry, of all things, then stopped and felt that I should open the door. I started an inner dialogue, What? Open the door? I don't want to. I don't want to know what's going on behind that door. Yet, I somehow mustered the courage, found the key, and opened the door.

I pushed the door open to see his thigh exposed and a needle buried into his skin. I would find out later that the syringe was filled with heroin and cocaine.

I remember reeling, using the doorknob to steady myself, my mind trying to register what was happening. My entering was a total surprise, and he swiftly gathered his clothing, ran down the hall, and locked himself into another bathroom. It was strange, but at that moment, I was completely calm and confident in what I was about to do. I felt no emotion, only solid determination. I walked down after him, lightly knocked, and he answered back, muffled behind the door. The message I relayed was life-altering for all of us, "Pack your things. It is time for you to go."

I corralled all the kids into my Chevy Tahoe and headed to Boondocks Party Land, where they ran between the arcade games, eating pizza, and up and down the indoor playground. I was still inordinately calm, and as I was checking on my baby leaning over his stroller to dig out a fallen binkie, I looked over, and my soon-to-be ex-husband was walking towards me through the door. It was the first time I saw him clearly, sick and lost. So deathly ill, his eyes and cheeks looked sunken and hollow. His clothes hung off his body and shifted awkwardly as he moved toward me. "I need money. I am going out of town," he said. I wrote him a check, and he left, and I did not see him again for months. That was the day my personal transformation journey from the old to the new began.

I no longer accepted the impossible task of "balancing" my husband's addiction with everything I was trying to juggle. I began the journey of self-awareness that balance was a farce, and until I could find my true self and focus on my personal vision for life - all else would fail. At that moment, I stopped trying to do it all. When I said, "Pack your things," I felt a new feeling, a solid feeling. I felt in true harmony with myself. It was a sense of calm amidst the chaos.

My mind turns to you as you are now seeking harmony in your life. You are stepping into a new way of living. You are starting a journey focusing on the future, leaving the past where it belongs—in the past. You are the inventor of yourself, and you get to *put yourself first*. As you move through these pages, you will recognize your ability to set and reinforce boundaries and protect what is most important: your own life.

You are now beginning your journey to Life-Work Harmony.

CHAPTER 2

Orchestrating Harmony

*"Harness the power of the pause and redirect, which
puts you in your rightful role as the conductor of
your life."*

–TRINA CELESTE

I was only twelve, but it seemed like an excruciatingly long time to wait for a beautiful singing voice to develop within me; my daily prayers were never answered. So, instead of joining the chorus in seventh grade, I opted to play the flute in the school band. Since hand-me-downs were customary in our family of ten children, I inherited my older sister Darcy's flute and shined it up as best as I could. It looked close to perfect, other than some minor dings and dents, but the sounds which came out as I made my first attempts to play it were only hollow breaths. No music would emerge.

During my summer introduction to band camp, our orchestra conductor, Mr. Boone, with his often-disheveled comb-over, dressed in his standard cream butterfly-collared shirt and brown polyester pants, taught me how to make the music flow by placing the flute just below my bottom lip and breathing across the hole to create sound. I was determined to find my notes as Mr. Boone taught me the techniques for playing.

After school started, Mr. Boone mysteriously disappeared for a few days, only to reappear sitting atop an inflatable doughnut. He never explained why he'd changed his conductor's throne to this inflatable device, but we all made up hilarious stories about it being due to his hemorrhoid surgery. At least it was something funny to pass notes about, complete with extremely descriptive pictures.

Mr. Boone bouncily conducted our gang of musically-challenged students, interspersed with a few gifted players. We were a tribe of sixty fidgety, awkward, and giggling new musicians which somehow he managed to elicit harmony from, nothing short of a miracle. He knew where to stop and instruct us until we fell into line in a semi-congruent orchestra. His pauses to reset and teach provided the attention necessary for us to make corrections.

At first, we were lucky when we achieved a full five seconds of harmony, hitting each drumbeat on rhythm, notes in tune, with no one overpowering the other. But as we progressed, we improved. His critiques were constructive. I remember his wand would go from a calming back-and-forth wave to a sharp pointing stick directed at the chaos maker as his temper flared at our lack of practice or the high-pitched squeals of an off note.

I remember holding my breath at each of the halts, waiting for his sharp redirect to end. None of us wanted to be on the other end of that pointed wand. But he taught us something invaluable early on: *each failure is an opportunity to improve.*

My flute-playing progressed until I earned the second chair, never quite reaching the ultimate prize as first chair gold. But the memory of Mr. Boone's high perch on his air pillow and his ability to turn an inelegant group into a harmonious orchestra remains an inspiration today.

It reminds me that disharmony in my own life can be remedied as I learn to pause and redirect and take my rightful role as the conductor of my life, which we must take to maintain

Life-Work Harmony. Life is not a circus act, and we are not all performers on the tightrope of a work-life balance; we are the conductors of our life harmony.

TUNE IN TO CONDUCTING YOUR LIFE SYMPHONY

Are there areas in your life where you are in control and expertly conducting?

_____

_____

_____

Are there areas where you feel out of control, where others may be conducting your life?

_____

_____

_____

FINDING INSPIRATION

Before I had a family, my version of harmony came from immersing myself in multiple stimuli. It was often all high-frequency fun with friends amid the stress of school, finals, and working graveyard shifts. There were nights we stayed up late playing pool or poker. One of my friends had a massive Great Dane who had his own couch as a doggie bed. One evening, we laughed hard after his horse-sized dog jumped for a tennis ball and slid uncontrollably into a wall, putting a hole large enough to walk through. These gatherings and many others allowed me to let go of the weight of my worries by pocketing eight balls, stealing poker pots, or just sharing laughter while sitting on the grass on a summer evening.

On other days, the harmony came after satisfying my craving for rest. When a long weekend came, I would sink into the downtime, sleeping extra hours to refuel to push through the following week. Sleep and aloneness were my harmonies. My way of slowing the pace and allowing myself to tune into a lower frequency. But throughout my life, even more than these external factors, the harmony came when I got my head straight.

When I took time to pause and reflect on internal inspiration, I allowed my thoughts to influence my actions, projecting either good or bad into the world. Harmony and induced energy started to flow into me.

Looking at your own life, how are you finding time for yourself?

30 DAYS TO HARMONY

As you move through this book, set aside time for reading, contemplation, and building a better understanding of your true self. Chapters have been designed to be about a fifteen-minute read. I suggest allocating an additional fifteen minutes to allow your mind to wander, acknowledge feelings, write, and flow through your thoughts to find personal inspiration.

Identify specific times throughout your week when you will pause, change your pace momentarily, and tune in. As your harmony usher, I suggest doing one or two chapters a day in which you would then complete all elements to harmony within a month. These moments will motivate you to move forward with determined energy through each chapter and stay in harmony as you do your inner work.

THE PEACE GARDEN

Recently, I met with a group of life-first harmony seekers searching for a more holistic path to harmony. And because I believe nature is a great healer, and in nature, harmony abounds, we gathered at a local garden aptly named the International Peace Gardens. Here we paused and recentered. We connected person-to-person and heart-to-heart, sharing our paths and forging new ones together. We met to refocus and tune into a new vision for how we can manage our life and work in more harmonious ways.

When disharmony creeps into life, reset, redirect, and remind others to do the same. As this group of experienced professionals and return-to-work explorers gathered, they sought ideas on conducting Life-Work Harmony. I took a page from Mr. Boone's book, and we shared and evaluated individual experiences fostering opportunities for change.

But most of all, we gathered to find our version of harmony, listening for that undercurrent of music that will remind us we are meant to feel joy and peace, not chronic stress and anxiety. We gathered to pause and tune in to our true selves.

As we move down new paths toward harmony, I know this path will be unpracticed for many. We're not used to listening but rather to being swept up in the storms which come with life. We are so busy we rarely pause to feel the sunshine or explore our inner selves to find more effortless paths for our journey.

This is a reminder to pause, take a "time out," and to "tune in." Just like we put a child in a time-out when they misbehave, we need to take a break when we find ourselves in disharmony.

THE POWER OF THE "TIME OUT"

Write down times when you will take time daily to create personal timeouts. If you do not prioritize time for yourself, you will keep living someone else's priorities, not staying true to yourself and finding time to read, reflect, and recharge.

It may be 15 minutes here and there, or an hour, whatever works best for you. It may be going for a walk or locking yourself in the bathroom (which I have done many times at home and work) to find moments of peace.

Once you set time aside for yourself, prioritize it and protect it from other life demands.

TUNING INTO TIME-OUT

When can you put yourself in time-out?

Where will you go?

What will you do to help you tune in? Could you utilize journaling, meditating, or breathing techniques to assist as you take time for yourself?

RAISING THE BATON

At the Peace Gardens, many paths wind between diverse gardens planted to represent distinct cultures from around the world, each with its unique fingerprint, but all work together to create a beautiful outdoor space.

Hot pink penstemon takes turns dancing with yellow-horned poppies and ruby red asters flash their petals as we weave around one path towards the Japanese Garden. Two Thai monks garbed in coppery robes smiled at us as they meditated under a pergola. A Hispanic family met for a living memorial celebration, releasing dozens of purple and white balloons into the sky, floating effortlessly into the azure blue. It was a magical day; the air was fragrant with late summer blooms, and those who joined me were chatting quietly as we walked towards a grassy spot in the shade to learn more about the powerful concept of Life-Work Harmony.

The wonderful scent of possibility hung in the air as fragrant as flowers. We were stepping into unknown territory, forging a new path together, hoping for the possibility that life doesn't have to stretch us so thin. As a presenter of this group, I hoped to impart a portion of the harmony I have found as I learned to give up the balancing act and instead turned to harmony.

Our group gathered on a grassy hill under a Bonsai, feeling the weight and stresses of the day fall away.

"I tried for years to balance work and family," I share. "But once I became clear about my true vision, the universe responded."

Because we needed to start boldly, I asked them: "How many of you are attempting to balance work and family? Talk to me about it."

Stories came back, honest and sobering: about terminally ill children, divorce, moments of giving up careers for children, and struggles to find their way back into the work world after being stay-at-home mothers. Stories about how they felt like they were drowning and didn't have the luxury to put life first because they were single parents trying to provide emotionally and financially for young children.

I wanted to reassure them.

"We are going to stop seeking balance," I say. "Work-life balance is impossible, and the sooner we understand this, the better. Although we may feel a bit afraid of going out in the world with our wounds showing, believe me, this new way of going within and inviting harmony brings much-needed healing."

We stare down the myth of work-life balance, asking it to back away like a wild goat that crashes into our garden and wants to head-butt its way in and eat all we have planted and nurtured.

I raised the baton, eyes lifted and focused, pausing for instruction in finding Life-Work Harmony.

"Are you ready to feel it? Cue the heavenly choir sound effects. Just kidding, but can you hear the music within that wants to resonate? That wants to sweep you up into it? Can you feel harmony within, waiting to be tuned in and played?"

Heads nodded in the affirmative.

Harmony is hard to define, but most of us agree we know how it feels when we don't have it. Everyone uses a different equation to achieve harmony. As my kids say, we either "vibe" or we don't. The great thing about harmony is you get to create your version of it. You get to be the conductor, deciding what genre, instruments, and players you will invite! You get to choose the melody that will suit your needs.

Let me take you on visualization for a moment: Imagine your life as a garden, lush with green grass and sheltering trees. It can be a serene and happy place. A place where you allow yourself to stand at the center of planning, guiding, and architecting your ultimate life design. You can weed your garden, allowing only pleasant and nurturing thoughts to seed and grow.

These chapters help you identify how to keep your harmonious garden healthy and blooming. It is here where you get to dream and design your life outcomes. It is an effort in mindfulness, focusing inward where you can pause and recenter. Where you now reflect on what is growing well and what may need tending. Where you continually tune in.

Just as your garden requires continual care, you also require daily tending, fertilizing, turning soil, pulling weeds, keeping out unwanted pests, and ensuring you plant only those things that will reap a harvest. It is work that takes awareness, time, and focus. Without a clear understanding of yourself, it is easy to get distracted by doing things that consume your time and do not lead toward your end design. You will begin the work to tune in and center on harmony within your life.

TUNING INTO YOUR EMOTIONS

What are your thoughts as you consider this transition from balance to harmony?

Have you felt moments of peace, panic, or nervous excitement?

What emotions are you feeling at this moment?

CHAPTER 3

Finding Your Purpose

*"Focus to find your spark, gain clarity in your
purpose, and unleash your superpowers on the
world!"*

–TRINA CELESTE

In my senior year in high school, I ran for Homecoming Queen. I didn't know it then, but it would be an experience that unintentionally exposed my purpose early in my life. Just this year, I recognized the revelation of my life's purpose as I heard Big Audio Dynamite's punk/pop sound pump through my New Wave radio station. A purpose now embedded in my soul and finding its way into my daily actions: transforming lives through education and career transitions.

As I entered college, I originally began my studies in architectural engineering. I always deeply loved architecture and took drafting for three years in high school. In the pageant, I represented as a member of our Vocational Industrial Clubs of America (VICA). The club was predominantly male, and as the only female member, it was the first time VICA had been represented in the pageant.

Here is the comical but poignant setup for my homecoming skit. The lights come on stage left; I am dressed in a black and white maid outfit and cleaning the floor with a mop. My dad's baritone voice comes through a recorded soundtrack we had made on a tape cassette.

"Is your dead end stuck in a job? Is your rear going nowhere?"

Big Audio Dynamite's song *Rush* plays in the background, and on cue, its lyrics feed in.[1] The stage light pans right to my fellow companion, Craig, sitting at a computer deep in thought and typing away on a Macintosh, the screen glowing green. Wearing khaki-colored dickies and a button-up, he turns and stands, stretching his hand to me. I hold out the other end of my mop, and we swing around and do a cutesy little two-step dance.

Dad's deep baritone returns and says, "In VICA, you too can change your atmosphere and learn opportunities in Vocational Industrial Clubs of America."

The memory makes me laugh, but what is incredible is that I was living my purpose from a very early age. As I listened to Big Audio Dynamite in my car, I thought, "Holy $#*%! I have been transitioning people to educational paths for thirty years!"

I am not sure I would put on a maid's outfit to convey this message today (maybe if it would make the right impact). Still, I put on a killer suit jacket and say the same thing thirty years later as I speak to our state legislature, creating awareness on pathways that will transform lives, drive economies, and improve society by transitioning underserved groups into technical education and career paths.

Your purpose is in you and shows up in your everyday actions. It's where you draw energy to get excited or passionate. You aim to find that spark, gain clarity in your purpose and unleash your superpowers on the world! Aligning your life and work with your core purpose enables harmony.

---

1   Big Audio Dynamite. (n.d.). *Rush* [Recorded by Big Audio Dynamite]. Retrieved from https://www.lyrics.com/lyric/15754798/Big+Audio+Dynamite/Rush

TUNE IN TO YOUR ACTIONS

Do you find yourself drawn to certain activities?

Were there activities in your youth that may indicate your purpose?

Do you gain energy by performing these activities?

What authors, speakers, and content are you most drawn to?

How can you align your life purpose and your work together?

Once you start to find where your passions are, it helps direct you to your purpose. When you realize how much fuel and fire these passions give you, you find ways to put your purpose first. As you shift to aligning with your purpose, you will see that it will begin to reward your work and relationships. You will be more energetic and make better decisions about where to spend your time and energy.

After I finished speaking at an event on finding your purpose, a woman messaged me, incredibly excited that she had found her purpose and a new vision for her life. I was excited for her and asked, "What is your newfound purpose?" Her response was, "Quilting!" Oh wow, I would have never guessed quilting, not in a million years.

What's so special about each of us is that we each have unique gifts that we get to choose to develop and how we want to use them to impact the world. She went on to say, "I have always been nervous about sharing my love of quilting, but I can see now how I can teach what I saw as only a hobby, build a business, and help others learn all that I know."

There are things we inherently are drawn to and love. For some, it is a sport, a specific knowledge area, or a set of skills we have developed. My husband loves to read finance books, it's relaxing for him, and our bedroom is a library of some of the greatest minds in finance, surrounded by Warren Buffet and Ray Dalio. I read finance books to gain knowledge and help me better run my business, but I am not often eager to pick up a finance book and read it for fun.

My bed stand is filled with books like *Mindset* by Carol Dweck, Brene Brown's *Daring Greatly* and Angela Duckworth's *Grit*. I love that we can all take charge of our lives and grow! I eat it up and can't get enough, yet my husband tires quickly on these books and instead scans for the quick wins and golden nuggets. There is no right or wrong in what we choose as our interests; the goal is to identify what they are and focus our time and attention on areas of strength.

TUNE IN TO YOUR INTERESTS

What are the books, podcasts, or media topics you are drawn to?

What people and events do you most gravitate toward?

What skills or hobbies do you have that get you excited to share with others?

THE PURPOSE TO IMPACT HEATMAP

Harmony starts with you. Your life, your needs, and your goals come first. It is not selfish to better understand yourself and your personal goals. Even more, you cannot protect something you have not defined. You cannot ask yourself why you feel disharmony and find an answer if you don't know what harmony would be for yourself. The first step in your work will be self-reflection and creating a personal purpose, vision, and values statement.

In 2019 I was diagnosed with breast cancer, and the coming months were some of the most deeply reflective moments of my life as I faced my mortality. Experiences like these force you to consider what is most important in life. This time of introspection was a gift, as I learned to let go, focus on positivity, and determine what was most important in my life. After recovering from a double mastectomy, I decided to return to school. And not just any school; I wanted to go to Harvard.

I have learned to respond when I get these "sparks" of thought. So, a month after surgery, I applied to Harvard Business School. I was accepted, flew to Boston, and completed a Driving Corporate Strategy certification. I eagerly soaked up the time and opportunity to learn directly from the professors who had written many of the Harvard Business Cases I had studied during my graduate studies.

At the end of the program, our global group of executives met for dinner. A fellow student from South America, Roberto, and I sparked up a conversation. He reflected on setting vision statements to drive alignment and focus on results. The conversation drifted to my recent cancer battle and how it had redefined my thoughts entirely on my future.

I remember sharing a new idea: "I have begun to see my life like a heatmap."

I explained that I thought of my life like an image of a map on a computer screen, with colors adjusting as I interact with individuals in my life. You can see all those you have impacted either positively or negatively. They are spread across the map in red, yellow, or bright blue splashes.

On my life heatmap, red signifies that you have hurt someone, been angry, or have unresolved contention. Yellow signifies indifference, ignorance, or a "not my problem" attitude. Blue is where you have had a positive impact leaving a bright, happy, what I like to call "Trina power blue" on the screen. This is how I see my life now, where I can see the impact of all those

I interact with and influence, either positively, negatively, or indifferently.

Roberto grinned, and his eyes lit up. "Yes! I so feel this stirring deep down within me. I want to be able to make an impact, but I haven't known how to give it focus."

Most people desire to leave a meaningful legacy in their lives. We want to impact those around us positively. We want to change the world for the better. We seek to give back in time and knowledge, where all our work, passion, and purpose align.

Businesses that clearly understand and communicate their vision and corresponding values more effectively accomplish their goals. We, too, must create our vision, purpose, and value statements, just like the dozens of business cases we had reviewed over the prior months. We had studied numerous vision and value failures, like the infamous Wells Fargo sales fiasco, where the bank fired approximately 5300 employees between 2011 and 2016 due to fraudulent sales. At that moment, it clicked.

When your vision and personal values are not clearly defined, you risk being improperly interpreted by others and influenced by their priorities. Let me repeat this because it's so important:

> *When you don't clearly understand your vision and values, others may misunderstand them and try to influence them according to their priorities.*

Some may have an inkling of their purpose but need a clear personal vision to guide them. Vision statements help you stay on course. They help define what success looks like for you, and we will develop your vision statement in future chapters.

Your purpose is your mission in life. It's derived by seeking things you are drawn to, giving you energy, and driving you forward. It is used to clarify why you are doing what you are doing and will inform you in making decisions about what you will or will not do.

TUNING INTO YOUR IMPACT HEAT MAP

Take time to reflect on those in your life you can positively impact. Take a few moments to reflect on your interactions with those in your circle of influence, where you are red, yellow, or blue.

Circle the color you feel within each of the relationship areas below.

IMMEDIATE FAMILY:	Red	Yellow	Blue
EXTENDED FAMILY:	Red	Yellow	Blue
FRIENDSHIPS:	Red	Yellow	Blue
WORK COLLEAGUES:	Red	Yellow	Blue
COMMUNITY:	Red	Yellow	Blue
NEIGHBORS:	Red	Yellow	Blue

Could you extend out any of these areas and list specific people coming to mind where you can shift from red or yellow to blue?

You may want to take a more active role in the community or a non-profit to extend your impact reach, stop the deep red gossip or speaking negatively about a neighbor's son who is struggling and instead reach out to see how you can build a friendship, or engage more with a son or daughter who may be drifting along in yellow haze.

Consider your relationships and how you can shift your impact map. If you like, you can do this on a separate piece of paper to write down a list of names. Then use a colored pencil or marker to highlight each one in whichever colors resonate for you. You may have "Sindee's super Sienna," "Chris's courageous Cyan," or "Maggie's masterful Magenta." Make this your own personalized and powerful color impact heat map.

TUNE IN TO YOUR PASSIONS, SKILLS, AND VALUES

Reflecting on your passions, skills, and values will help you learn more about yourself. Review the following discovery questions in these three areas to navigate you through finding your purpose.

1) PASSIONS

What are you passionate about?

What gives you energy?

What tasks do not feel like work?

What recurring activities do you see yourself doing in your life?

2) SKILLS

What strengths do people say you have?

What skills do you currently have?

What skills do you want to have?

How do your skills enable you to fulfill your purpose?

What jobs and activities are you frequently drawn toward?

3) VALUES

What do you value about yourself?

Here are a few personal value statement thought starters; add as many as come to mind:

- I value my skills and knowledge
- I value my physical wellbeing
- I value my mental wellbeing
- I value my spirituality

What do you value related to family?

What do you value as being great relationships?

What do you value in financial wellness? Do you value your time?

As you construct your purpose, stay at the center. Do not put your kids, work, spouse, family, or friendships at the center of your life. Valuing yourself first is what will help you stay centered in orchestrating harmony.

Your purpose should not say,

"My purpose is caring for everyone else."

"My purpose is to be a good parent."

Many people are parents, and parenting has inherent value in our lives. However, parenting is not your life's purpose. Instead, think about who you are deep down and what you care about outside of your role as a parent.

What specifically do you see you have to bring to the world?

What skills and passions do you have that you can put into action?

The answers to these questions create clarity and mute any external noise as you understand your true purpose. Your purpose gives you your "why" and meaning that will be a reinforcement when things get hard. Purpose empowers you, strengthens your resolve, and boosts your boundaries. Ultimately, your purpose is one of the foundational blocks as you build a tower of tranquility. So let's get building!

Your Value Statement

It is time to write your personal value statement based on your reflections in this chapter. Remember to include your why and mission; it excites you and gives you energy as you create an impact in the world. Use the following format:

My MISSION is, and will DO WHAT because I
VALUE what?

Here are a few examples for you to consider as you define and write life's purpose:

EXAMPLE PURPOSE 1

To use my passion for social justice and advocacy to create a more equitable and inclusive world for all.

EXAMPLE PURPOSE 2

Empower women to embrace strengths, overcome challenges, and lead confidently and authentically.

EXAMPLE PURPOSE 3

To inspire and educate others through my creative pursuits, using art and storytelling as a tool for connection and transformation.

My purpose is:

_____

_____

_____

_____

CHAPTER 4

Tuning Into Your Life First

"Tuning into yourself first puts you in the conductor seat where work no longer dictates your life, but your life dictates your success at work"

−TRINA CELESTE

O ver the last few years, my speaking engagements shifted from leadership to requests on "work-life balance." In preparing for these events, I recognized I could not tell any of these companies or their employees that "balance" was an option.

I am intentional in my choice of words in moving from balance to harmony, and the ordering of the words signifies a shift from carrying it all to living intentionally. In no longer refer-ring to work-life balance, but by transitioning to a LIFE FIRST approach, we find *life-work harmony*. When you place your life and priorities first, you gain control. You are fortified with a knowledge that enables you to act (not react) to your emotions and determine your best outcomes. ***Work no longer dictates your life, but your life dictates your success at work.***

In the spring of 2021, a year into the drastic reality of covid, I presented at Overstock's Women's Summit. My keynote topic was "Work-Life Harmony." Jonathan Johnson, Overstock's

CEO, kicked off the conference, and we had a few minutes before I took the virtual stage to chat about this concept of shifting from balance to harmony in our lives. He shared that when speaking to employees in their Ireland office, they use the phrase "life-work balance," not the more normal "work-life balance."

This subtle shift in placing the wording order of life before work into daily practice has an impact. Putting our life first changes everything. We begin to focus on those things in life that are most important to us, search for solutions, and set a vision for how we want our lives to be.

I hear this uncentered message often in the work I do with students. One woman stated, "I am working three jobs because I need to make so much to pay for everything. But I struggle to find time for my family and don't enjoy these jobs."

Attempting to shift her mindset from what she thinks she *has to do* to one more centered on her goals, I inquired, "What do you want to do? Forget about what you 'must do' let's get to what you would like to do."

"I would like to spend more time with my family, but I still need to make (X amount). I am not willing to give up my financial security and do have to pay the mortgage."

We then discussed shifting focus from the "must do" to a "big picture" vision. This shift helps you prioritize what truly is necessary and most important. Take your skills, match them to your desired job, and then identify the steps. You seek specific clarity on the expected salary and define the action plan to get there. Part of this envisioning process helps you determine which roles may provide the life integration you seek with family, friends, and hobbies.

When we reach the end of life, no one says, "I wish I would have worked more." However, the need to be able to provide is the trump card that enables other areas in life. Your primary driver is typically to make money to pay the mortgage, food, and care for yourself and your family. To find harmony, *adjust your thinking about work to one where it is part of your life and an enabler for your life's goals*—not in constant opposition to your life.

Sit with this idea for a moment more,

> *Work is part of your life and an enabler for your life's goals.*

Managing life gets simpler, and decisions become easier because you have clarity about your life's goals. Transitioning your career to meet your life vision is emotionally triggering. It can be challenging as you drop a perceived sense of safety, get uncomfortable, and move onto the right path. However, when you do, boom! The sense of clarity and direction you have created gets easier as you align to a new vision with a renewed purpose.

TUNING INTO YOUR LIFE FIRST

Begin the journey to center your life on you. Identify your wants and your needs and center on what is most important. You are not being selfish by being clear on what you want to achieve in life, and centering on yourself is a critical part of finding harmony.

Take a moment to reflect on where you currently are centered in your life:

Where do you find you are putting yourself first?

Where do you find you are often conflicted, putting others' needs before yours?

How often do you find time for yourself?

ESCAPING "THE BOX"

Have you ever found yourself trapped in a role that brings you unhappiness? It's as if someone has confined you to a box that doesn't fit who you are. You desire something different, but the pressure of others' expectations and the fear of judgment confine you within those walls. This often happens when individuals conform to gender norms or take on responsibilities that weren't their first choice. When you try to break free from these barriers, you encounter resistance, criticism, or dismissive attitudes that crush your attempts.

This feeling of being boxed in can occur at work or home, with family, neighbors, or friends who require you to present a version of yourself that doesn't align with your true identity to be accepted. It may come in direct or indirect messages telling you that you should conform to fit in.

The symptoms of being trapped in this boxed-in scenario are a sense of dissatisfaction and unfulfillment. You may have chosen a path of success based on societal expectations rather than your true desires. It could mean being stuck in a career you despise because everyone else believed it was the right choice for you. It could manifest as presenting yourself as the perfect spouse, the ideal parent, the reliable colleague, or the sibling who always comes to the rescue of others. If you constantly feel anxious and cautious around a group or individual, unable to relax and be your true self, chances are you are living within the confines of a box.

As a culture consultant at RizeNext, I've had the privilege of meeting remarkable individuals like Alan. Alan identifies as a black transgender male and has become a vocal advocate for LGBTQ+ awareness. His life has been a journey of navigating uncomfortable situations as both a black male and a transgender person. He describes it as feeling like people are trying to fit him into a box, and the fear of others' reactions pushes him to conform to social constructs that are at odds with his true self.

Alan's mother had the wisdom to send him to a private school, and as a young person, he became the first black student in an all-white school in Roanoke, Texas. Despite others' expectations, his ability to speak up and be authentic stems from his mother's encouragement to advocate for himself. Throughout his life, Alan has learned to reaffirm boundaries to dismantle societal constraints attempting to keep him confined within false constructs.

Alan had a disturbing encounter with the school's dean during his time in the honor society at the University of Dallas. She called him into her office and said, "You aren't one of them."

Confused, he asked, "What do you mean, not one of them?"

She replied, "You know, many black students cause trouble in the organization and don't finish. You are very responsible and different from them. Consider it a gift that you were able to complete your studies."

The shock of this blatantly racist remark was compounded by the realization that every person of color was potentially negatively affected by an unreasonable expectation of failure. The truth was that students weren't troublemakers, but rather the lack of support and the staff's biased assumptions hindered students' success based on the color of their skin.

This experience made Alan realize that people will hold their views regardless of their actions. He advises others to stop trying to navigate the expectations of others and echoes my advice: "Don't try to live your life in a box."

Recognize where the strings of others' opinions bind you to specific stereotypes or biases telling you you're incapable. Don't internalize these statements, and understand that these biased constraints can be untied or severed by living authentically. The more you dismantle these false barriers, the less power these boxes have to contain you.

Check your life's decisions to see if they may have been driven by societal norms, not your inner drive. You can begin to unwrap the boxes designed by outer influences and place yourself in the center of your life, trusting your imaginative designs. Take a brief moment to tune in and see if your purpose is being derailed because you are stuck in a box of someone else's design.

Has your purpose been buried because someone or something else took priority?

Do you see times when you wanted to do something but maybe held back because someone may not accept or judge you?

REFLECTING ON YOUR PAST TO DESIGN YOUR FUTURE

In 2018, I was conducting a keynote for an organization called Code to Success, which targeted High School students to participate in coding camps throughout the summer. In preparation, I was looking to find something that may entertain and remind individuals that they have a future in technology. The answer came to me, "You need to talk about goats and Barbies."

I am often asked, "What was it in your youth that may have led you to a career in tech?" My answer comes in response with three;

1) living my purpose

2) recognize my strengths, and

3) creativity and fun

In thinking about my younger years, I could have been considered outside typical gender norms. It has taken me over forty years to recognize that I had been finding my way outside of the boxes others expected me to live. I had been tuning my mindset to focus internally, then identifying and living true to my purpose.

BARBIES IN ACTION

As a young girl, I loved Barbie dolls, engineering, and design, all in no particular order. My Barbies would become extremely bored sitting around the Barbie house. You can only try so many outfits or decorate your house for so long before you get eager to get out and see the world! Unfortunately, or fortunately, my Barbies didn't have a souped-up pink Corvette like their friends. Instead, they zoomed around in custom-built motorized cars I designed and built from erector sets.

One thing my parents did right was provide me with toys that allowed me to explore my nature for designing and building.

I built powerboats for bath time and motorized cars so they could come with me on my outdoor explorations. These early models were most likely the first makings of Barbie ATVs. My Barbies had no issues getting their clothes dirty, and I now zip around on a dirt bike and play a grown-up version of Barbie motocross.

In 2020, I had the opportunity to meet Tan France, a fashion designer icon from Netflix's *Queer Eye*. My friend thought it funny to introduce me to him as "Tech Barbie." She asked later if she had offended me, and my reply was, "Absolutely not!" What better than to be recognized that you can love art, fashion, design AND engineering? It is wonderful to mix the enjoyment of all things considered feminine, like clothing, makeup, dolls, and technology. Why we think of these concepts as mutually exclusive to one another is a sham and a shame.

We all have things from our youth that signal us who we are, and as we have grown, they have developed into what gives us purpose. Often, they lay dormant, hidden away until we are exposed to activities that allow us to discover these interests. They appear as we move into our careers, start families, develop hobbies, or engage in community activities.

When speaking to university students, I often pose the question, "Were there things you did as a child that sparked energy and excited you?" The answers are always varied, but come across with excitement and enjoyment as they reflect on how they used to build rockets out of cardboard boxes or tear everything apart in their home to discover how they worked or how they loved doing "science projects" using every ingredient from their mothers' kitchen cupboard. Each of them an indicating hint of life's purpose and where to find energy and enjoyment.

TUNING INTO YOUR ENERGY

Let's take a moment to tune into your life's deepest passions. A treasure hunt, if you will, of adventurous self-discovery.

Are there areas in your life where you have found energy and excitement?

When you look back on your life, are there times you are drawn to the same activities?

What gives you meaning and energy? Is there something where it no longer feels like work, and the time spent feels rewarding?

REFLECTING ON LIFE EXPERIENCES

If you look back, you find purpose through repetition in your actions. As a child, I would count steps and push to see if I could walk the stairs faster. I would look for ways to design my room and organize and reorganize my books and shelves. I would measure and look for optimizations and methods to become more efficient.

One of these ways involved our family livestock, as we had a small family farm with cows, chickens, turkeys, and goats. One of our goats was named "Casper the Unfriendly Goat" due to her all-white coat and ice-blue eyes, which gave her a ghost look. However, this goat was not friendly; like most goats, she was extremely ornery, so the name was especially befitting.

I would rope up a red-rider wagon tying behind Casper, lacing it under and around her bloated belly. She would fidget and bleat while I tied her to a tree. I would then put my younger jovial brother Mike, age five, into the wagon. He was always eager to be part of my shenanigans. I suggest he owes me his career pathway in information technology since he always participated in my experiments, usually as my lab rat, learning to conduct and analyze the data we recorded.

This experiment entailed me untying Casper, slapping her on the rear end, initiating a bleat, and her racing off across the yard. My brother would scream "Yahoo!" and be laughing as I watched his chubby body and soft brown curly-queue curls bounce across the grass in the wagon behind her. I recorded each race and measured how long it would take before the wagon tipped, spilling my brother out and bouncing him across the green grass.

I would chase down the goat, gather my brother from the lawn, and we would do it again. We repeated the experiment, logging my findings on how long it would take before my brother would tip, bounce, and roll. I had to have a sufficient sample size to confirm the variance and outliers, and my early days of Six Sigma were at play as I worked through probabilities of success of making it from one side of the yard to the other.

These repeated "experiments" were the early days of efficiency planning and design thinking. We all have things we do on repeat and are the hints of where we may find the most success.

In a Harvard Business Review publication of Nick Craig and Scott Snook's article, From Purpose to Impact[2] their research shows less than twenty percent of leaders understand their

---

2   Craig, N., & Snook, S. (2021). *From Purpose to Impact*. In J. Smith & J. Doe (Eds.), On Managing Yourself (Vol. 2) (pp. 1-13). Cambridge, MA: Harvard University Press.

purpose. Yet, business experts argue that purpose is the key to exceptional performance and better well-being. You can find your purpose by reflecting upon where you are continually drawn.

We know we each have a purpose, but only a few know what it is, how to find it, or how to put it into action. You can become more aware of things you are continually drawn to that give you an energetic buzz and excitement. These activities often do not feel like work and will not leave you drawn out after engaging.

TUNE IN TO YOUR LIFE EXPERIENCES

Do you ever hear comments from others about your passion?

Were there life experiences that were particularly impactful to you?

Are there any life history hints that provide insight toward your purpose?

CHAPTER 5

Creating Your Life Vision

"Powerful change happens when you recognize the gravity of a situation, envision a new path, commit to it, and take action."

—TRINA CELESTE

VITTLES TO VISION

When I finished high school, my plans of cruising into my newfound freedom ran into a significant snap: I found myself riding fifteen miles down and back up our steep canyon road on my little brother's bicycle to work at a fast-food restaurant called "Vittles." My driver's license had been revoked due to three speeding tickets, a car accident, and an improper lane change. It was a dispiriting experience, and I was mortified to find myself sliding around on greasy floors and arguing with my co-workers about whose burger order was who's. I was at a crossroads, unsure of where I would go or what I would become.

The reality of my situation escalated one day as I cruised down the canyon road and hit a puddle. I lost traction, and my bike and I landed into a four-foot-deep ditch overrun by weeds. The impact was quick and hard. After regaining my breath, I peered back through the long grass up over the edge of the ditch in hopes no one had seen my fiasco. My gaze was returned by an older woman in large bottlecap glasses in a silky pajama gown and slippers holding a garden hose. The trickle from her hose was now watering the sidewalk as she stared wide-eyed across the street at me, her ancient voice rasping, "Sweetie, are you okay?"

"Uh, sure, I'll be okay," I told her, heaving my bike out of the ditch, tearing at the thick grass caught in the chain and wheels, my ego wounded. The sting of the deep scrapes on my elbows was not the reason tears welled in my eyes. My emotions all hit simultaneously, driven by thoughts that I may be walking to work and would now be late and that I couldn't lose this job. I wanted to be in college but needed the Vittles dollars I was trying to save to get into school. Mostly, I just felt like a stupid girl caught in this ridiculous circumstance by the all-seeing gaze of this little old lady.

I straightened out the handlebars as best I could and rode the rest of the way to work. I am not sure if it was this actual day or one shortly following that I made the concrete decision while sliding around on those greasy floors, "I will not live this life."

I saved my Vittles dollars and entered my first semester at a local state college in architectural engineering. My love of architectural design stemmed from years of watching my father at a drafting table designing and building steel structures. He was a dreamer and a builder, and his trust in others in business led to business growth and failure. The resulting impact would be that my nine brothers and sisters and I had moved ten times by the time I was fifteen.

I loved school. Education was my saving grace in life, and I will always be a massive proponent of knowledge in any format to transform. I had been able to pull enough money together to get into that first semester. My first year of school was just the opening of the dam, and since then, the waters of knowledge have never stopped. I took architectural engineering, structural engineering, and electrical engineering, and my coursework required a Pascal programming class that would forever change my life and the lives of hundreds I have worked with who have now created their transformations into the world of technology.

I enjoyed all forms of engineering. It was here that I was introduced to the beautiful world of "computer science;" in 1996, it was not yet called "high tech" or "technology." It was something new and bold and sparked something within me, and I knew I needed to be part of it. Recognizing that drafting was not a highly lucrative career and that becoming an architect would require the same time as a doctorate, I switched my studies to computer science.

I did not want to continue living in my hometown and was searching for a new start. A review of job service positions resulted in one that allowed me to go to school during the day while working the graveyard shift at Hill Air Force Base. It was an hour away, but it gave me enough distance to find some autonomy, but not so far that I felt disconnected.

I didn't sleep much during those years of completing my computer science degree. Honestly, my sleep deprivation did not result in the nicest of demeanors, but it was wonderful, as I was now on my way to a new vision and version of my life.

You get to determine your path, a new future, and it is one full of immense possibilities! In these moments, you can stop to pause and recognize, "I am not in the right place or heading in the right direction." You begin to realize you are no longer a victim of your circumstances and can instead take control. You may fall, have to pull yourself out of the ditch, reattach the chain and get going again in these times of failure where you get to reflect and forge a new vision for yourself. It's exciting to step back and redefine who you are and where you want to go.

TUNING INTO YOUR PERSONAL VISION

Do you have a current vision for your life? What is it?

If you do not have a vision for your life, what ideas come to mind about how you would like your life to be?

Write down all ideas that you would like to see in your life. Do not go small; go big!

What would you do in life if you could do anything?

VISION, COMMITMENT, ACTION (VCA)

In 2016, I worked for eBay as a Senior Manager in their CX Technology Operations organization. We had a leadership off-site, and I was set—or so I thought—to fly to San Diego. When I showed up at the airport, I was informed that the travel agency had canceled my flight and no more flights were available to San Diego that day. I was stranded at the airport; my husband, having just dropped me off, had to circle back again to pick me and my bags up off the curb.

I was annoyed and frustrated, returning home in an irritated huff with the travel agency that had canceled my flight without notice due to an incorrect name. I was unsure how it made sense to try and still get there in time for the kick-off. Once home, I sat watching the NBA playoffs. But I couldn't relax, feeling strongly that I needed to go.

I called multiple airlines, and it was the same answer. "Sorry, there are no more flights to San Diego today." I could have given up again, but then said, "Okay, what flights will get me close?"

"Los Angeles has a flight that would get you in at midnight."

"Okay, let's do it," I told them. I rallied my husband, and we went back to the airport. I found a car service to drive me the hour's trip at midnight to my hotel.

When I think about this day, I'm so glad I persisted. The next morning the keynote speaker was Cathy Burke, a senior leader at The Hunger Project, or THP, an organization working to end world hunger. She spoke on how the leaders in ending hunger were people experiencing poverty, mainly women, who had been locked out of any decision-making role in their villages. THP has profoundly changed the lives of millions of people by understanding and acting on the principle that "everyone is a leader." Her team understood that to see real change in the world, you must empower and provide knowledge to everyone, not just a select few.

There is such power in just showing up. I didn't realize it then, but listening to that inner voice telling me to fly to L.A. and showing up that morning would change my life drastically. At the end of her speech, our SVP stated that eBay would be doing a leadership program in partnership with THP and would send a few leaders to a "to be announced" location. As he said this, I thought to myself; *I will be going.*

The thought wasn't, "That sounds interesting," or "What a great concept." It was a solid "I WILL BE GOING."

Three months later, they announced the details of the program and opened applications to thousands of workers within the company. I submitted my application, and when they called to inform me, they said, "Out of all the applications, yours was the one we knew should be going. No question."

I shared the news with my co-workers and family that I would be traveling to Senegal, Africa. But this moment was when the doubts began to set in.

My manager said, "Do you know how many shots you will have to get?"

My mind said, "Oh crap, that's right, I have to get shots! Dang, I didn't think about that." It was a lot of shots, seven to be exact.

Next was coordinating the family. My husband and I were married for a year, and the dust was still settling. Blending a family with eight children was a never-ending roller coaster of chaos. Ensuring our kids would be okay for ten days took serious coordination. I worried about malaria, time away, and traveling into the unknown. But I pushed through each mental barrier shouting at me not to go and would pause to reflect, returning to the affirming thought that came to me that day, "I will be going," and held firm to my commitment to participate.

This experience propelled my work in helping individuals become self-reliant through education and career development. It has been one of the most transformative experiences of my life. As I flew to Senegal jet-lagged and dragged my bags across the parking lot to an awaiting car I knew I was where I was supposed to be.

After arriving in Senegal, we met that first morning to learn how the organization works in Senegal to help people become self-reliant. They shared a model called VCA—Vision, Commitment, Action. Cathy was sitting at the front of the room, her dark hair and light skin offset to a bright blue dress, Indian-influenced patterns reflected in highlights of green birds ready to take flight. She shared, "VCA is a process to facilitate a mindset shift in people to take their destiny into their own hands. From an attitude of resignation, towards one of 'yes we can' and newfound self-reliance."

THP is an organization of only three hundred staff, yet it has brought millions of people worldwide into their leadership so they can feed themselves and their families. The VCA workshop was the starting point for this, and the start of the VCA is about setting the vision.

The VCA model applies to anyone seeking change and harmony within their life. If you desire to achieve change, an open mindset is required where you become aware of any limiting beliefs and release any resistance to change, applying your commitment to transform your life. This is an opportunity to reset and strive for new desired outcomes and a willingness to understand things do not have to be as they are.

In the ten days I traveled throughout the sands of Senegal, my understanding of the growth mindset became more cemented. Carol Dweck's work from *Mindset: The New Psychology of Success*[3] pushes us to look at situations as temporary and suggests that you can create change. Dweck states, "In a growth mindset, challenges are exciting rather than thinking, oh, I'm going to reveal my weaknesses, you say, wow, here's a chance to grow." You are not helpless. You are the creator of change in your life,

---

3   Dweck, C. S. (2006). *Mindset: The New Psychology of Success*. New York, NY: Random House.

and seeing challenges as opportunities for growth allows you to take responsibility for your own life.

For those working with THP, there were shifts in mindsets from, *"If you are born poor, you will always be poor,"* to a thinking pattern, *"I may be born limited, however, my future is limitless."*

As we entered villages, we would visit epicenters developed to support the communities as they worked toward self-reliance. They would cheer us on entering, at times young children singing and clapping as they walked up the sandy walks into the cement buildings. Other times, my heart would be filled as we were welcomed by drums beating in courtyards of villagers dancing, including us in their celebrations of self-reliance for thousands of their community. As they banged out rhythms on buckets and bowls, we would join in dancing with strangers as we moved our way forward into the center of the village.

In the evenings, I would continue to hear the drumbeats playing in my head as I lay down to sleep. My eyes closed, laying under a mosquito net, I was no longer worried about malaria, the shots, or my responsibilities back home. A smile would appear on my face as I would reflect on the life changes they had created. All it took was someone to help them determine a new vision for their life, a mindset shift in understanding they were now in control, no longer dependent on the charity of others.

One villager in the Sanar Epiceter briefly shared his newfound understanding that we are capable of much more as we broaden our minds stating, "Knowledge is our money."

You have an access card to the library of awareness of how things could be, and there is a power within you capable of envisioning and bringing to life massive change.

The number of stories and life alterations increased as we moved from village to village. Changes in healthcare, agriculture, new homes built, and kids in schools all started from what they called "mobilizers" who would go to their villages and share the vision conveying, "It is time to change."

When visiting the Sanar Epicenter, we were introduced to Mr. Felix, one of the most dynamic people I have ever met. Breaking out in song, he would get people laughing, dancing, and singing at a moment's notice. His ability to recognize and leverage his personal strengths made him a great leader. Using his ability as an artist to draw people in, he would say: "Everyone likes music," and create entertaining events to pull people in and then share his vision of a different future.

He shared a message and story of his challenges and opportunity to change. He had wanted to learn agriculture, so he attended training on farming. "I am not sure if I am a good or bad farmer, but I can learn," he told us, showing us his large farm of beautiful cabbages, grains, and vegetables. He would "test and learn" with fertilizer, starting small, learning, then adjusting as he went until he would get it right. As he worked to build his gardens, he said, "Mistakes cannot be avoided all the time."

You, too, can test and learn. You are never sure when you get started if you are good or bad at anything. However, you will never know unless you start. This is the power of showing up, getting started, beginning with a spark of interest, then fanning the flame as you dig in, learn, adjust, and grow.

Mr. Felix's ability to mobilize people came from engaging with interest, creating clarity, and setting a new vision of how things could be. "You need to talk about the seriousness of what is going on. Help people recognize the seriousness of their situation for them to be open to the vision of what could be, commit to change, and take action to change the situation."

You may need to consider the seriousness of your situation. Gain clarity on what is working and what is not, and be honest about where you are now and how you envision your life in the future.

TUNING INTO YOUR VISION

What knowledge do you need to reach your vision?

What challenges are you facing that may prevent your vision from becoming a reality?

Who do you need to engage to reach your life vision successfully?

What strengths can you use to help drive meaningful conversations and change?

Are there conversations that you need to have to realize your vision?

What concerns do you have in discussing your vision with others, and how can you mitigate them?

TUNING INTO YOUR VCA PLAN

Let's now create your Vision – Commitment – Action plan.

VISION - Create a clear vision statement

Taking your earlier reflections, define your vision statement. It should be a clear and specific picture of what you want to achieve and your desired outcomes. It involves setting long-term goals or objectives that are inspiring and motivating.

With newfound clarity, you can manage your boundaries, staying focused on suitable activities and saying no to the wrong actions.

You'll utilize your statement to allocate time for those activities that will lead you to your vision.

COMMITMENT - Personally committing to your vision, reinforcing your fence lines, and strengthening your resolve.

Commitment involves making a dedicated effort toward achieving the vision. It requires a willingness to make sacrifices, persevere through obstacles, and stay focused on the goal.

Your ability to make decisions with commitment exemplifies courage.

When committed, you speak with understanding and can ask the right questions, striving for knowledge, enabling you to take action toward your goals.

ACTION - Focused actions toward your vision.

The action involves taking steps toward achieving the vision. It consists in creating a plan, setting milestones, and taking consistent and deliberate action toward the end goal.

Remember that you most likely will get pushback as you try to enact changes. Expect to be tested, challenged, and pushed on your ideas.

Being persistent and transparent in your "why" will help you navigate and respond.

PUTTING VCA INTO ACTION

Take time to revisit your VCA plan frequently.

Print it out, place it on your bathroom mirror or bedstand, or tape it to a wall where it is visible. As you revisit your plan (weekly is suggested), look for areas you can enhance and where new priorities have arisen.

Where do you need more time to develop your VCA plan?

Learn more about The Global Hunger Project at thp.org, and visit the trinaceleste.com blog for images and expanded stories.

CHAPTER 6

Propelling Your Vision Into Action

"When your vision aligns with the world's need for positive change, be prepared! It is only a matter of time before the universe sends the reinforcements required to make your vision a reality."

—TRINA CELESTE

In 2019, a knock on my front door opened the gate to establishing Tech-Moms. I answered, and my neighbor stood smiling on my doorstep, her short curly hair radiating in a halo backlit by sunshine. Her hot pink lipstick contrasts her white and green broad-striped shirt, and she says, "I want to work. How do I get started?"

I asked her in, and we sat in white wing-backed chairs, discussing her situation and what had prompted her to walk over. "I am tired of not working and want to feel fulfilled. I hear there is so much opportunity in the tech industry, but I feel overwhelmed." I know now that she isn't the only one feeling this way, as all of our students have had that same spark of interest, yet a previously invisible path prevented them from taking steps forward.

The idea for a technical skills and career development program for adult women had stewed for years, but this visit propelled me into action. I firmly understood that women are eager to enter the technology workforce, but the doors were shut, and their knocking had been going unanswered. I had a glimmer of insight into how much this knowledgeable source of talent was going untapped, yet no one else was doing anything about it.

Over my career, I had grown tired of the immediate response from fellow managers as we reviewed candidates seeking more diversity, "Women just don't go into tech." (Goatsh*t!) The direct prompt I needed to move into action was sitting directly across from me in bright pink lipstick, and I could no longer ignore it. My response to all those who had easily disregarded women as capable came to a head, and it was decided, *Fine. I'll go freaking create them.*

I began making calls and sharing my vision with everyone I knew. One of these calls led me to my friend Scott, and he and the universe, connecting me to my cofounder, Mikel, and eventually to our third cofounder Robbyn. It has been a whirlwind since we aligned our visions and passions, and we have now placed hundreds of women on the tech pathway.

Mikel had gone through a similar program in Silicon Valley and was interested in bringing it to Utah. Together, we held nightly meetings, Mikel from her San Francisco flat and Robbyn and I from our Utah home offices. We shared our vision, built plans, and hit the ground running in fundraising, connecting with technology companies, and collaborating with higher education institutions.

I was working full-time and had to temporarily carve out evenings away from family and reallocate them to our new vision. We were clear in what we were about to do, who it would impact, and the benefit it would bring to those companies who for years had been stating, "We can't find enough technology talent." They had been overlooking what was right in front of them, a massive concealed pool of talent ready to be put into action.

The intrusive questions we had along the way were never-ending, "What if we get shut down by a global pandemic?" "What if we don't get the funding support?" "What if we can't make the impact we are seeking?" Ignoring these internalized and verbalized questions of doubt, we held to our aligned "why" and built one of the fastest-growing educational non-profits in the state.

To transform your vision statement into a reality, begin imagining all the possibilities. Forget the "What if this happens?" Or "What if I can't?" or "I don't have such and such that others have." None of that matters here as you get to dream and ask, "What do I want for myself?" Focusing solely on you and your ambitions allows opportunities to manifest as you work toward your vision. You get to be self-interested! And I guarantee you are super interesting.

Create a clear statement by starting with the end in mind. What does success look like? Is it a strong, happy family? Is it a life of great experiences and memories? Does it include a career that allows you to create those experiences and provide for your family? Does it include continual learning and being fulfilled by your personal growth?

Be authentic and be true to yourself. Examine what you write, and ask yourself, is this genuine to me, or am I providing the correct answer according to someone else? What do you envision happiness is for you? Who gets to be involved in your life, and who doesn't?

TUNING INTO YOUR LIFE'S VISION

We will start with the "big picture" and then step back to the present. When you envision the end of your life, what do you want to look back on and say, "I did that!"

Who do you want to see has been in your life?

✗ a partner-
✗ Family

How do you want to have changed the world?

- I want to leaves stories
For people to cherish

What do you want to have built?

- a house where
people can come and
go and I can
feed Them.

Which relationships are going to matter the most?

Family,
partner

What do you want people to say about you?

- kind compassionate,
Funny, determined,
successful unflas

How do you want to make people feel?

- loved ♥

How will you feel?

- Ready for next chapter

Will you be healthy? - yes - do yoga and swimming

eating well - fresh garden

What are your interests?

- Literature - music, art, nature, The Ocean, languages, traveling

What are your finances like?

- no debt - enough to travel w/out worrying

Most often, if you fast forward and examine what you want, it will include your family, close relationships, experiences, stability, and impact. Rarely do we say, "I wish I would have worked more hours or had more things." You could live in a way that nurtured your soul and those around you. You will have stable finances and could care for others because of it. You will want to have built things that make the world a better place for current and future generations. Think big! Be bold! Have fun dreaming of all the fabulous things you will do with your life!

TUNING INTO YOUR LIFE'S MEANING

This next set of questions will get you started dreaming of the future version of you. Draw a large 'X' across a piece of paper, then outline a square, signifying the fence lines around your life's harmonious garden.

Envisioning Your Future

Center yourself in it, then ask the following four questions in each area of your garden.

1) What, or who is truly meaningful in this area?

2) What seeds would you like to have planted now for future harvest?

3) What actions will create the most abundant growth?

4) What does your final flourishing garden area look like?

Envision Your Relationships

l have good boundaries
l am not dating
new people, l have one
life partner

Envision Your Financial Health

I am free of debt

Envision your Career and Community Engagement

I have a rewarding career - That doesn't leave me depleted every day.

Envision Your Personal Health

- I am exercising - summary - eating well

VISION TO ACTION EXERCISE : START / STOP / CONTINUE

Be cautious not to bring any negative past into a new vision of your future. There may be things you don't want in your life any longer. You may continue poor habits or harmful engagements if not identified and removed from your life.

Throughout my career, I would do a quarterly start/stop/continue exercise, evaluating what worked in our day-to-day efforts and what was not, and what needed to start, stop, or continue. I would write everything we were working toward on the board and determine what needed to be done to ensure we could meet our goals and drive results.

In the same way, you can utilize this exercise when you feel overwhelmed, exhausted, and burned out. Stopping to tune in and inventory where you're spending your time helps identify where you can make adjustments.

Journaling daily helps create visibility of where you are feeling strained. For those that use a daily calendar, do you over-schedule yourself? I recall many marathon days in my career where I had done over thirteen meetings in a single day! How is that ever productive?

Prioritization lets you focus and helps you decide what is most critical and aligned with your goals and vision. To help create perspective, you can ask yourself what you may need to start, stop, or continue:

START: Is there something you should start today that enables your vision to become a reality?

sacrificing financially

— apply for meaningful jobs

STOP: What are you doing today that you should stop, as it is not leading to your vision of success?

— online dating - stupid guys
distraction -
I should focus on ONE person who share values

CONTINUE: What is working well in your life that you want to continue?

a personal routine of writing and exercising
Quiet meditative time

CHAPTER 7

Committing to Your Why

*"Propel your life past wishy-washy living. There
are no wrong paths when you are decisively moving
forward toward one vision."*

−TRINA CELESTE

A t the beginning of classes, I work with students to clarify their vision by writing down their "Why." Why did they show up that day? Something sparked inside them that got them there, and we spent a brief moment tuning in and recalling what that was.

When the days get long, life throws challenges your way, or you get stuck on a problem and want to give up, you must remember WHY you are doing it.

Understanding your *why* will get you to show up when you want to stay home and watch that new Netflix series. It keeps you plugging along, leading to additive experiences and the incredible joy of accomplishing and overcoming! You gain a sense of fulfillment in seeing your growth from where you were to where you are now. Personal development is exhilarating but is only found after the work has been done.

There are no wrong paths. The wrong path is the one that is untraveled, never started, frozen in anxiety, fear, busyness, or distraction. You will learn and grow on every journey that you take.

In writing this book, I have gone back to my why daily, sometimes hourly, as I pushed myself into action, staying focused on why and to whom I am writing. In 2021, I was messaged by someone I had never met, only having connected on social media. His message said, "Can you come to my office?" Odd, I had known of Randy, an influential businessman, author, and well-connected individual that lived just a few miles from my home. I agreed to meet and scheduled a brief meeting. As we sat in his office, we got to know one another, as he shared his background and experience, I did as well. Then he said to me, "I feel prompted to tell you, you need to write your book." My first thought was, *Uh, what book?* The way he stated it was like I had already had a book in mind ready to go. I had been asked about whether I had a book before, but had always responded, "I don't want to write a book. I don't have the time."

I have been published in magazines, written thousands of technical articles, and built a curriculum for decades, but writing a book was daunting. Randy prodded further, "You need to write your book." He held up a book by an author he relayed was a friend, Mel Robbins, and said, "You should be doing this."

We finished our meeting, and as I was leaving, business entrepreneurs revolved in and out of his office, and I met several as we finished our time. His seed had been planted, and I began internalizing the idea of writing a full-fledged book. That week, six more people asked me, "When will you write your book?"

My mind relented and committed to myself; *okay, fine then, I will write a book.* But first, I had to figure out why I wanted to write this book. I had one critical problem; I had yet to learn what I would write about. I didn't have a single purpose in mind, and I had no idea how anyone writes a book, but I started. I picked up the phone and inquired with those I knew who had journeyed down this path.

As I put thought and focus onto the idea of a book and created a vision of what I wanted this to become, it came to me that the vision and why for this work would be to *help anyone struggling to find "balance" in their work and life be able to achieve harmony.*

It has been over a year and a half as I pushed through this work, along with various other priorities in my life, and ironically, I have continuously utilized what I am writing about to achieve my vision. The seed was planted by my friend Randy, however, it was watered and fed as I went back to my *why*, giving me the motivation to continue efforts toward its completion.

TUNING INTO YOUR WHY

Are there projects you have had floating around in your thoughts you have yet to put into action?

Has anyone told you, "You would be great at..." and you have not responded? _write a memoir
of dudes lie dated._

What meaningful projects would you like to do, and why would you like to accomplish them? _finish my 2 Nobels_

THE "COMMIT AND SHIFT"

Many of our students become extremely excited as they learn about all the various opportunities. As they gain exposure to multiple visions of what that could become, they start dashing down several paths simultaneously. It is a typical response to feeling like you need to educate yourself in *all things* before committing to move forward on a single track.

I recall working with a student whose story was of too many commitments. She was getting a project management certification, going to school to complete a college degree, attending an online boot camp to become a full stack developer, working full-time, parenting, and was burned out. She had been learning about various roles available and began to engage in not just one role but started taking multiple higher education learning paths. Short stints like this can be done, and she eventually completed all her goals, but only after she recognized she needed to focus.

She paused her time in her boot camp and focused solely on her degree. Once she finished her degree, a company hired her, and she was able to focus on finishing her larger vision of becoming a software developer. She shifted, restarted her online boot camp in the evenings, and completed this next goal. When we spoke, balancing it all was taking a detrimental toll on her mental and physical health, and she was on the verge of quitting it all. Instead, she stepped back, selected, and committed to a single initial path.

Attempting to over-educate and execute simultaneously creates burnout and the likelihood of ineffective distraction as you try to harness too many things. There is nothing wrong with getting excited about all the opportunities in life! However, over-allocating ourselves across multiple endeavors at once will not bring harmony. Pick a single career or development path and commit to it. Focused attention to a clear way partnered with knowing we are continuously learning allows you to build upon your skills and knowledge one step at a time.

When you can't confirm which pathway you are on, you are being what I call "wishy-washy." Pick what is currently the most beneficial path toward your vision, and then shift it later.

Commitment to a single focus is powerful as it enhances the productivity of your utilized time. You should not tolerate any "wishy-washy" approaches to life. You can become caught in thinking, "Oh! I could do this, and this, and this..." By committing to a single clear vision, you can more effectively realize your dream.

You may also be concerned if you think your vision, plans, and priorities are right.

You think, "What if I get it wrong?" or "What if I go down a path and have to restart?"

All these are normal thoughts but can paralyze you from moving forward.

Understand, there is nothing wrong with starting with a single vision and then shifting. You can shift at any time and then commit to the next set of actions. Opportunities will come while on the journey. They occur in the knowledge you build, the skills you develop, and the relationships you create.

Stay committed to your vision. It should be the priority, and everyone else's priorities will fall by the wayside. No more attempting to "balance it all."

Commitment to yourself, and your vision, will empower you to say "no" when necessary.

"No, I can't manage that event."

"No, I cannot start another project."

"No, I have other responsibilities right now."

Commitment also allows you to identify when you should say "Yes!"

"Yes, I will take that leadership position."

"Yes, I will go to the gym."

"Yes, I will set aside time to study each day."

The clarity in our vision, purpose, and priorities allows you to stay focused and on target for your life's renewed vision. You have now put your life first, and in doing so, you committed to the path of harmony.

TUNE IN TO YOUR COMMITMENTS

Where do you see that you may be spreading yourself too thin?

Do you allocate yourself to multiple projects?

What is your primary commitment?

Using the *Life-Work Harmony Model* daily will help you determine where you may lack care in your life and will help you create plans to cultivate harmony. This chapter will share ideas to help you tune into harmony while planting for future success.

We will take moments to pause, tune in, and find where disharmony may be occurring. As we continue, pay attention to the terminology, and apply it to your life.

Light, Air, Water, Nutrition, and Space, or L.A.W.N.S, is a simple acronym I learned in an elementary science class that can be easily adapted. No single area works independently; they are interwoven, and when internalized and integrated, they will help you orchestrate your version of a thriving harmonious garden.

GETTING OUT OF THE WEEDS

As a single mother, I traveled internationally for work. I lived in a nice area with a beautiful large yard with garden beds throughout a three-quarter-acre lot. I loved the space and would spend hours weeding, planting, mowing, trimming, and caring for my yard. Although it brought me joy, it also created intense exhaustion. Tending to all the demands of the gardens became increasingly overwhelming, and as the hours added up, the weeds multiplied.

One day, upon returning from the airport, I pulled into my driveway and was overwhelmed by the thorny weeds growing out of control. Some weeds towered over my head, consuming and hiding the shrubs and flowers beneath. I remember that day well because my garden felt like a reflection of what my life had become. I had not kept up with the weeds, which were now overtaking the gardens and my emotions.

I sat in my driveway staring at the neglected brambles, which seemed to laugh at me as if they were growing taller by the second. It felt like they were coming to strangle me. I couldn't take it—caring for my three young sons and fighting to keep from losing myself in a tangle of conflicting demands and impossible weeds was overwhelming me. I had nothing left to give as they blocked any glimpse of my garden, and I broke into exhausted sobbing.

It wasn't only the weeds in the garden; weeds of anxiety were growing inside me, fed by the emotional burden of my divorce proceedings. The weeds were of panicked fear at the reality of tumbling losses sustained in my real estate investments after the 2008 recession. Then there were the weeds of immense guilt when trying to explain to my boys why their father was no longer visible in their world. There seemed to be no way to continue to provide for my family while carrying these heavy emotional burdens.

After my divorce, I was lost in the weeds of parental responsibilities, running a household, caring, nurturing, supporting, and providing for my family while working full-time. Somewhere in all this, I had lost myself. I was consumed by emotional weeds and suffering from complete exhaustion.

Weeds of fear, doubt, shame, and guilt were sprouting and spreading everywhere. Whether real or perceived, they were taking over my life.

I fantasized about walking into the garage, grabbing a red gas can, dumping its fluid onto those malicious weeds, striking a match, and watching them go up in bright orange flames. I shook the thought off and picked up the phone to share my destructive thoughts with a friend.

I could always rely on getting a reality check from my dark-eyed and level-headed friend. She firmly said, "You need Freddy."

I called the number she gave me to schedule Freddy, the head of the local lawn maintenance and gardening crew whose services provided me with additional precious time. My "pause and phone a friend" helped me understand that we can't do it all, nor should we. She was saying, "You need help."

I am not sure why I hadn't recognized that it was okay for me to get help. I had an incorrect notion that I was required to prove I could do it all. Despite the hell I was going through, I kept up the appearance that I was thriving. I put on a smiling clown face, showing everyone I was strong enough to balance this ridiculously precarious tightrope and juggle everything. Trying to do it all left me empty.

The feeling of seeing those beautifully trimmed gardens was incredible! I let go of this false idea of "balancing it all," but it didn't stop with my yard and garden. I began looking for additional opportunities to LET GO. *Getting help isn't just something we should do, it's something we must do.*

The few dollars I spent were worth every moment of relief I felt every time I came home after Freddy's crew had been there. Gas can fire fantasies were replaced by moments sitting outdoors reading or watching my sons play Power Rangers among the trees. Instead of pulling weeds, I planted flowers. I found moments of harmony, no longer feeling guilt or pressure to balance it all.

It's not easy creating a vibrant, harmony garden in your own life. It takes practice and work, self-care, and nurturing. You should be tending daily to your life's garden as you require continual planting, watering, and weeding. You may get discouraged at times, but I want you to know that part of the journey is to face challenges, to stand in the middle of weeds, wondering where your beautiful garden went, and then begin step by step to get back into harmony.

I invite you to wander in a garden to pause and think about harmony and the natural state your garden is in. Consider the following areas in your life, and how much are they adding or detracting from your health and happiness?

- **LIGHT** represents your *family and relationships*, which provide you joy and can be the sunshine of your life when tended to appropriately. You exhibit care for yourself by removing toxic relationships that prevent light from entering your life.

- **AIR** represents your *financial health and wellness*, an area frequently neglected and left in disarray with inattention. Financial wellness is the calm breath that comes when all are attended to or a subtle breeze that accelerates the spark in any other areas of your life for good.

- **WATER** represents your *work, career, and community* involvement. This is where you can find fulfillment through your aspirations, achievements, and contributions. It is an initiator for growth as you put yourself into harmonious action.

- **NUTRITION** represents the fertile soil of *mental health and wellness*, which grounds you and is from where all else grows. Strong psychological and physical wellness will maximize your life's growth.

- **SPACE** represents your *personal development.* You must create space for yourself, allowing your life to come first. Find ways to invest in your skills, hobbies, spirituality, and personal knowledge to tend to your overall growth.

Below is a simplified visual of your garden and its structure in a well-tended and manicured state.

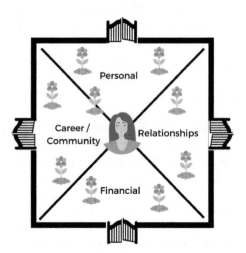

Put you at the center of the garden

Although *Nutrition* comes fourth in the acronym, it is of the utmost importance in enabling all other areas within your life.

You start with the fertile soil of mental health and wellness for all else to grow. Your emotional state determines your ability to invest time and energy in family, relationships, finances, work, community, and your ability to focus on your development.

Depression and anxiety can be a symptom of other areas not being tended to or may be clinically derived and should be attended to before all else. In future chapters, we will discuss keeping your mental soil in good health.

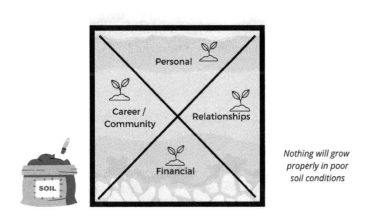

Fertilizing the soil of mental health

YOUR DAILY HARMONY CHORE LIST

1. Nutrition first. Fertilize your mental soil. What are the potential areas where you may be mentally malnourished?

2. Begin to envision your life's garden through the lens of the LAWNS model. Think about what you want to plant in each area and what you should remove.

3. Schedule time to tune into the harmony you want to flow into your being. Setting time each day lets you tune into what is working and what is not. Are you able to quickly identify which areas need tending?

CHAPTER 8

Keeping Out the Goats

"Keep out the goats that consume, and invite in the gardeners that bloom."

–TRINA CELESTE

A few years ago, I rediscovered a favorite book by James Allen called *"As a Man Thinketh"*[4] in a little bookshop in Maui. As I reread it that evening, sitting on my hotel balcony, listening to the waves crash into the shore, I did something I now do with every book I read and altered the gender references to the female form. And as I read "As a Woman Thinketh," it took on a new powerful meaning. The words now spoke to me, not someone else.

I quote with these gender adjustments.

If you are a man reading this, note how difficult it is to relate to this message without the proper gender reference. I do not make these adjustments to exclude anyone but to create awareness of how often women have felt when reading texts exclusively told through the male pronoun.

Allen writes, "A [woman's] mind may be likened to a garden, which may be intelligently cultivated or allowed to run wild;

---

4   Allen, J. (1903). *As a Man Thinketh*. The Project Gutenberg EBook. (Original work published 1903)

but whether cultivated or neglected, it must, and will, bring forth... through creative power, [she] may command the hidden soil and seeds of [her] being out of which circumstances grow, [she] then becomes the rightful master of [herself]."

Men, consider how this felt. Did it feel relatable to you? Reread with a change in gender reference. Is it different? This is why gender references and pronouns matter.

We begin your work from the inside, pulling out your weeds of doubt, fear, shame, guilt, anxiety, and negativity and then planting the seeds of positive thought, which bloom into joy and beauty. Within your garden, you are doing either one of two things.

1) Tending and planting that which can grow and bloom, or

2) Ignoring and neglecting that which makes your life fall into disarray.

James Allen shares, "The outer conditions of a person's life will always be found to be *harmoniously* related to [their] inner state."

Your outer circumstances should never control you. Instead, gain control by focusing on your vision by centering on your purpose, creating clarity, and setting personal priorities you take control of.

SETTING THE FENCES AND CONTROLLING THE GATES

You protect the various aspects of your life by setting **boundaries** and making intentional decisions based on your priorities. Besides tending the garden, you must care to the reinforcements surrounding it: your *fences* and *gates*.

Through the remainder of this book, you will learn how to grow and maintain your harmony garden and mend and set your fences. We'll talk about boundaries, who is crashing them, and how to reinforce them, which is where talk of pesky goats comes in.

KEEP OUT THE GOATS!

The homes I was raised in sat in the valleys along the base of the Wasatch Mountains of Utah, always surrounded by mountains towering on our home's east and west sides. At each of our homes, my parents would plant expansive gardens, which became my places of refuge, the place that always felt safe and centered and where I spent countless hours in the summers planting, weeding, and playing.

The garden was my place of work and play. I would sit among the rhubarb, picking and eating raspberries and watching the fast-growing threads of string beans wrapping their vines along the lines. It was playtime after we finished milking the goats, feeding the turkeys, and pulling our allotment of weeds.

You should be able to take refuge in your garden, and it's your space to develop, grow, and build rewarding relationships, career success, and financial wellness. You should hold your life sacred and protect it at all costs from those trying to deter you from your vision for your life and future.

I frequently recall my mother's daily chore list reminder, "*Close the gates, and keep the goats out of the garden.*" (If they ever got in on my watch, I would be on toilet scrubbing duty.) This childhood checklist rings true for our non-literal goats. Creating a chore list helps you stay free from distraction, distress, disharmony, and possibly toilet scrubbing.

As we move through each chapter, you will become more aware of those people in your life who are the goats and those who are gardeners. I use goats as a metaphor for those activities and people in our life who consume because that's what goats do. Some individuals do this intentionally, and others I consider as unintentionally insensitive. Either way, you need to be aware of who is consuming so you can set the fence lines and control the gates.

You may have had goat bosses who were not about the team, only caring about their career progression. You may be spending time trying to please a goat, assuming they are a gardener. No one is trained to identify goats and gardeners, yet once you dig into looking at individual actions, you begin to discern the goats from the gardeners. Question who is there to help you grow and who may be there to consume.

Goats attempt to push and prod through your gates, eating and consuming everything they can get, leaving you with piles of goatshit to clean up. *You must learn to say no.* Goats consume what you've planted and nurtured without regard when you do not control the gates.

Our family has a high desert mountain ranch, and we spend time annually walking the fence lines and mending gaps where cattle are crossing. The beasts forage water sources and trample valuable vegetation when fences are unattended. As you venture down this new Life-Harmony path, walk your fences frequently, building and mending as you go, preventing the overconsumption of your precious life resources. Then, invite those willing and capable of helping you achieve your vision through the gates.

TUNING INTO MENDING FENCES

Have you set fences to protect you from distractions that would keep you from achieving your priorities?

physical fences w/

And if not, where do you need to mend your fence lines?

Is it in time, relationships, financial wellness, work boundaries, or creating space for yourself?

relationships
and
financial wellness

Did you have fences at one point and then allow them to fall into disarray? What happened to them?

Financial fences →
I was careless - also missed
being there so I got
parking tickets home -

KEEPING OUT THE GOATS: REINFORCING OUR BOUNDARIES

I often hear, "I am afraid to say no," the discomfort of turning someone's request away is too much to face for some people. Instead of facing the fear, they allow their time and energy to be trampled. Fear of building fences may stem from an unnatural feeling of saying no. If this is you, it may come from years of socialization that you should always give.

You're saying yes, even if you want to say no, which could also result from a lack of energy where you defeatedly give in because that seems easier. This may be because you are in disharmony elsewhere and are staring at an old fence that has fallen that you're too tired to repair.

Within your fences are *gates*, and you are the controller of the entrances to your garden. You decide what you will allow in and what should be kept out. Manage your time and protect your energy by focusing on your priorities.

When you give all your time to areas that are not in your master plan, you quickly become overwhelmed, anxious, and feeling unfulfilled in your life. Disharmony ensues, and you find yourself chasing goats instead of growing your garden.

TUNE IN AND REINFORCE YOUR FENCES

Where are the gaps in your fences, and who or what goats are getting through?

spiritual - D.s.

- doubts about meeting potential

- fears

Where could you shut the gates to control your time and energy?

- tackle to D.s. - tell him
Boundaries

Is there anyone or anything you need to close the gates on? Toxic friends, relationships, or a workload which leaves you with too little time or energy for yourself?

- expectations for job of society

STANDING IN THE CENTER OF YOUR GARDEN

Now that you have set the fence lines and have functioning gates, let's recenter you amid your garden. What words, emotions, or feelings come to mind that feel most harmonious to you? _ love, laughter, trust, energy, connection, inspiration community, nature.

Reflect on when you have experienced moments of joy.
- laughing w/ sister about reception videos
-

When have you been in flow? Where were you?
→ swimming 2 days ago
→ being in the ocean
→ writing my Novel
- teaching sunday school
- laughing w/ sisters

What was the circumstance?

What demands did you have to remove to get there?
- Be with family
- Be in Familiar territory

Think about when you felt most in control and stable; when and where was this?

A LIFE HARMONY MEDITATION

As a suggestion, use the meditation below to center yourself. There can be a benefit to getting out and allowing your mind to wander. Wandering in a garden, going for a walk, or an activity in an outdoor space helps provide a visual reference.

CENTERING IN LIFE HARMONY

Imagine you are standing at the center of your garden.

Birds are chirping, and the sun is shining giving you warm comfort.

There was recently a rain, and the air is fresh.

There is a slight breeze that rustles your hair ever so slightly.

You are safe.

The fences are strong, and the gates are shut.

The world is patiently waiting for you to decide what you will open yourself to next.

After reflecting, write down twenty words that evoke and activate a sense of harmony in your life. This list can be used as you move through the coming chapters to find your personal harmony.

CHAPTER 9

Nurturing the Soil of Mental Wellness

"Just as a gardener cultivates [their] plot, keeping it free from weeds, and growing the flowers and fruits which [they] require, so may [they] tend the garden of their mind, weeding out all the wrong, useless, and [mixed] thoughts, and cultivating toward [excellence] the flowers and fruits of right, useful and [refined] thought."

–JAMES ALLEN

AUTHOR'S NOTE: *In addition to changing the gender form, I have removed from this quote the words* **pure, impure,** *and* **perfection.** *Women often are pushed to unrealistic expectations of "purity" and "perfection." I invite you to eliminate these words. Shift your thinking away from the idea that perfection is the goal and that your worth is connected to your purity, thus defining you as a person. Instead, focus on* **personal development, ambition** *toward excellence, and ongoing* **refinement** *as goals.*

These last few years have highlighted the necessity of attending to and reinforcing mental wellness. Consider the burnout of athletes like Simone Biles, who stepped away from opportunities to achieve Olympic gold due to extreme stress and anxiety, which gave rise to her now-famous words, "It's okay not to be okay." It is a revolution in progress when we recognize that our mental health and wellness can no longer be neglected. Remember, our mental health is the fertile soil in which all else grows; without it, we fail to succeed in other areas of our lives.

After her historic move, Simone worked to make it her life's mission to help others focus on their mental wellness, taking a role for *Cerebral* as their Chief Impact Officer and advocating for young female athletes. She is not alone in seeing the challenges the world is facing in battling depression, anxiety, suicide, and a sense of unacceptance for anyone who is not presenting themselves as perfectly happy.

According to the Centers for Disease Control and Prevention (CDC), in 2020, suicide was the twelfth leading cause of death in the United States. It is deeply concerning that it is the second leading cause of death, behind unintentional injury, among individuals between the ages of 10-14 and 25-34, the third leading cause of death for ages 15-24, and the fourth for ages 35-44. In 2020 there were nearly two times as many suicides (45,979) in the United States as homicides (24,576).[5]

Our family's challenges with mental health and depression had existed since before I was born, never having met my grandfather, who was lost to suicide, or my great-grandmother, who left this world leaping from a bridge. There are pictures of my grandfather hanging on the wall in my home, a vibrant man, handsome, polished, sitting in a suit and fedora hat, leaning against a horse-tethered wagon.

I often reflect on these pictures, seeking to understand what may have been happening underneath all the big smiles and larger-than-life personalities. I have pondered their lives while

---

5   Centers for Disease Control and Prevention. (2021). WISQARS Leading Causes of Death Reports [Data Brief]. Retrieved from https://wisqars.cdc.gov/data/lcd/home

looking at black and white photos of him and my grandmother at the beach, their hair blowing slightly in the wind and laughing faces. In one cherished picture, he has a rake in hand, bare-chested in a bathing suit working in his massive gardens along the Snake River in Idaho. He is poised ready to take a break with a refreshing dive into the cool river water.

I am learning and slowly developing an increased understanding as I work with my son as he battles his mental health challenges. My son has a similar frame and build as his great-grandfather, Jesse, and his long journey has led me down a path of self-discovery. I cannot fully understand the struggles of many; however, I can attest to the burden I have seen with people I love and am grateful for their willingness to draw back the curtains and look within. Their shared stories provide us with broader hope as we build awareness and acceptance of challenges surrounding mental health.

LOSS OF MUSIC

In September 2020, I was awakened from a deep sleep by my twelve-year-old son saying, "Mom, my dad is on the phone."

I was confused. Why would my ex-husband be calling at this time of night? I took the phone in a fog and hoarsely said, "Hello?"

"Skye is in the hospital," said my ex-husband on the other end of the line. I responded, "No, he is downstairs asleep." My mind did not grasp that he was not asking a question. I raced to think if I was mistaken about him being safe downstairs. I recalled him going to bed in the evening, walking down the stairs, and me telling him, "Goodnight, love you."

He continued, "He called the suicide hotline, and they instructed him to walk to the hospital."

I sat straight up, still so confused. *He's at the hospital? He's not safe downstairs? He was going to attempt suicide!* I thought it was all a bad dream.

"I'm on my way," I responded, my chest welling in fear. In a fearful panic, I leaped out of bed, telling my husband I was heading to the hospital and would call once I knew what was happening, and I rushed out the door.

My urgency was halted as I walked in the hospital doors, where due to Covid restrictions, I was directed to wait in a spaced-out line. What felt like hours was fifteen minutes before they let me into the emergency room. I raced to my son's bed seeing his slightly lean body outlined under a thin blanket. His immense blonde waves surrounding his head were in elegant disarray. He lay in a curled position, his blank stare looking through me. My relief came as he moved slightly, and I asked, "Are you okay?" I touched him, but he bound himself tighter by pulling away.

The doctor joined us and informed me he'd been admitted for suicide watch. He continued, "He has been planning on taking his life and was saving his medication for months." My mind went blank, unable to consume what had just been shared, my heart ached, and my stomach turned over in waves. The thought of the pain he must have been feeling for so long brought tears, so I took short breaths to keep from dropping to the floor.

I looked back at Skye, and he made no attempt to talk. I gave him space and discussed the next steps with the doctors. I called to inform my husband that Skye would check into an in-patient center at the University of Utah Mental Health Services. I did not know for how long or what was to come. As I ended the call, I could only say a statement of intense gratitude, "Thank Heaven. He is alive."

My mind went to the months leading to this life-altering moment. He has always been the "easy kid" I didn't need to worry about. The one that would do his homework, practice his piano, and eagerly dig into a literary novel. As a child, he would come to me from the moment he could walk and talk, saying, "Mom, I am going to sleep," and head off down the hall to get in bed as I followed him, tucking him in with a soft kiss on his forehead. I never had to potty train him. Never a single accident or urgent rush to use the potty. His logical progression presented itself by saying, "I am ready to wear big boy pants."

It was his self-sustainment that may have misled me for so long. I didn't pay sufficient attention, noticing that the long hours buried in literature masterpieces may not have been good or that the electric piano with headphones in his room had gone quiet. His prior pervasive music was no longer being brought to life.

For the next three weeks, I traveled the hour's drive back and forth to the mental health center, visiting for brief periods. Unskilled in this new format of scheduled communication, we began to get reacquainted. The first day I arrived after checking him in, I went to hug him, and he pulled away. He refused to be touched. As I looked into his eyes, I could see the music that was once within him was nowhere to be found.

His eyes were empty, averting to look anywhere but at me. He sprawled on the couch, and as we attempted to visit, he slowly sunk lower, his body becoming noodle-like, and he ended up with his head on the arm and the remainder of his body somehow split between the seat of the couch and the floor.

"Tell me what has been happening?" I prodded, my body bracing for the answer. He informed me that his depression had slowly increased over the last six months. He felt nothing; he cared for nothing, not even me. "The only thing that makes me feel emotion is thinking about my little brother 'Z.' Nothing else is there."

He paused momentarily, and we sat quietly. He continued, "The pain of feeling nothing is too much to handle. I want it to be over." I broke hearing these words, but floodgates held back internal sobs, and I was afraid I could never close them if opened.

I visited the series of specialists, nurses, and doctors that would be serving to help my son over the coming weeks. I met with his counselor, psychiatrist, patient coordinator, and others, each adding various insights and perspectives to this new world of mental health. I learned the importance of reinforcing his great reaction and behavior by calling the suicide hotline. I applauded him for making that call, confirming that this was the right thing to do as he was about to end his life.

Inside, I was a complete wash of horrified emotion at the thought of *what if it had happened? What if I had walked in to find him that morning?* It was too much, and I pushed the thought aside. I asked a series of questions, "What are the next steps? How do I best support you? What should I say? What don't I say? What is the likelihood of recovery? Is this lifelong?"

I was getting pushed farther and farther into awareness of how many people and their families suffer. I watched the number of patients coming in and out from the lobby. I learned what clothes I could bring, "no drawstring pants," as they can be used to strangle themselves. "Do you have a gun? Is it locked up?" The questions responded to with a flat yes or no, again each time pushing the thought of these possible situations from my primary consciousness.

I took a few days off from work and found that my absence was not good for me. I got all my affairs in order and called my boss, sharing what I was going through. He was calming. He was concerned and incredibly empathetic to our family's needs, informing me that he had worked as a student on the suicide hotline and understood my pain. His awareness and support were welcomed, and I returned to work.

I had taken a position at Oracle as a Senior Director of Consulting and, for six months, had been building a new strategic accounts organization. Recognizing that I could do little at this point and knowing that Skye was in experienced hands, I moved my mind to something other than imagining finding him lying on the floor of his bedroom.

I worked from home and could take breaks in between meetings when needed. These brief breaks offered the respite required to handle the following contract review, budget forecast, or client call. At times, I would take a "time out" and lay on the floor next to my office chair, shutting my eyes and allowing my mind to flow wherever needed.

Progress was slow with Skye. I wanted answers and someone to explain why this was all happening. It never came. Skye did the work by attending group meetings, personal counseling sessions, and meeting with his team of doctors. He began learning behavioral skills allowing him to manage suicidal ideation and recognize passive versus active thoughts. I would look for the music to return each visit but never saw it ignite.

At the end of his program, we checked him out with strict instructions from his counselor on what to do once he returned home. It was again a new set of triggers and fears as he would go to bed each night and the fear of what may happen while I was sleeping. We agreed on a new system of check-ins, me asking, "On a scale of one to five, how are you feeling today?" If it was a three or above, it was good. If it were two or below, we would be on watch.

PRACTICING SELF CARE

We began to get into new rickety routines as Skye returned to school. We were only at the beginning of our journey to wellness for all of us. We had been so focused on Skye and his well-being that my husband, kids, and my well-being had taken a back seat. I was still in shock, and it wasn't until I began seeing a counselor that I realized that I was dealing with a form of post-traumatic stress syndrome, or PTSD.

The thought that I should be dealing with my issues or taking time for myself was something I had never considered. It was Skye who was sick and at risk; however, I was waking in panic every morning for months and driven down the stairs in complete panic to knock on his door and make sure he was still alive.

My counselor, Amanda, was insightful, explaining the impacts of experiencing trauma, and that the heavy load I was continuing to carry wasn't required. I had been so worried about Skye, my family, and how everyone else was feeling that I hadn't taken the time to realize that it was taking a personal toll on my mental health.

The idea that I could just let it go didn't seem plausible, yet I leaned in as she explained while sitting cross-legged in her chair, a stack of papers on her lap, taking quick notes while asking me questions. Her head was shaved on one side and dyed in deep hues of purple and blue, counterbalanced by mousy brown waves grazing perfectly on her alternate shoulder. Looking intently at me, she inquired, "What do you fear? How would it feel to let that go?"

I visualized a feeling of being without the fear, without the nightmares that had been plaguing my rest. I answered these questions, and tears ran down my face. I was at odds with myself, thinking it was okay to let it all go. My incorrect assumption was that if I let the fear go, I would not be responsive enough, and he may take his life, that somehow my fear was keeping him alive.

We continued our work, and she began conducting EMDR (Eye-Movement Desensitization and Reprocessing), or rapid eye movement treatment. Pausing and counting while she quickly flipped her pen back and forth after introducing new thoughts of freedom from fear and pain. Like a conductor's wand, her pen introduced new melodies of view in my mind, replacing my initial fears, which were plucked and thrown out. We played the tune multiple times, and she would ask, "On a scale of 0-10 how disturbing [or distressing] does the incident feel to you right now?" Each time, my number dropped lower and lower, and I began to feel more and more at peace.

A new calm settled over me, and I no longer felt the emotion carry me to extreme thoughts of death. Hope now existed where I had felt we were at the mercy of the seeds of depression planted in our DNA, handed down from generation to generation. I no longer had to accept the lack of control of life-destructing bulbs rising in our soil, year after year. I no longer stood helpless or reacted to the extreme at the knowledge of my son battling suicidal thoughts. Instead, I slept. I didn't wake in a panic, rushing down the stairs to see if he was alive. I allowed things to be and flow naturally as we continued to heal.

CONTINUING THE SEARCH FOR TRANQUILITY

Over the months, we saw moments of laughter and brief glimpses of hope, but they did not last. After six months, he continued experiencing extreme thoughts of suicide. I began making calls, one after another, once again, attempting to find a psychiatrist willing to work with a minor who had openings in their schedule. My search went on for days without luck, and eventually, I connected with an outpatient mental health program. I applied, and after a few weeks, we put him in a center an hour's drive from our home.

He began a new series of work and treatments again with counselors, group therapy, and psychiatrists. They introduced behavioral methods to help manage his extreme thoughts. As he participated in his classes, I held doctor meetings between work meetings, filling my break times with treatment planning.

During this time, my parents contracted Covid and were treated separately at two different hospitals. The thought of the possible death of loved ones was a constant in my life. I was relieved to finally have a conversation with my mother after her release from the hospital. I had not shared what we had been going through with anyone, not my parents, friends, or family. I opened up and relayed details, albeit in abbreviated summaries, to minimize pain.

The challenges of suicidal ideation never just "go away." Skye's thoughts of *gunshots* and *death* are ones that we have agreed not to discuss in detail as it is too harmful to my psyche. Instead, he visits a counselor weekly, giving him a safe outlet to manage his thoughts and allowing him to process with an expert guide.

We each set personal boundaries with an understanding of what we need to keep our minds and hearts safe. We had open discussions, staying within our agreed borders and no longer hiding or reacting to his thoughts of self-harm. When appropriate, we granted ourselves permission to remove his mental health from being the primary focus allowing life to return to a natural rhythm.

Skye returned to his books; his music and notes rose from his piano, filling our home. As he played his latest favorite tune, *Where is my mind?* by The Pixies, we laughed, and we allowed life to be. At Christmas, his text request list for Santa read; "Jane Eyre, Lord of the Flies, Of Mice and Men, Frankenstein, Dracula, Alice's Adventures in Wonderland by Lewis Carroll, and The Brothers Karamazov by Dostoevsky."

His love of books is what saved his life. The dire night when he had reached his target date of inventorying enough medication was gratefully interrupted by a thought left by a character in one of his books, who had also decided to call the suicide hotline. The story left a lifeline that reached out and stayed within him, leading him to halt the creation of his "last chapter" and make a phone call to safety.

Our story is not unique. I too often hear stories of inner struggles related to personal mental health. Many are encountering this journey along with their loved ones, some are working with children as young as the age of eight battling suicidal ideation. There is a power in sharing our stories, and knowing that you are not alone.

The importance of finding harmony in society and within ourselves cannot be understated. Open dialogue and destigmatization surrounding topics such as suicide are essential in addressing mental health struggles. By actively engaging in conversations and breaking the silence, we create an environment that supports and uplifts those in need. Through awareness, support, and early intervention, we can work towards prevention and improved mental health outcomes for individuals at risk, fostering a society that values holistic well-being and harmony.

Awareness of our shared struggles allows for a healing connection as we find ways to combat life's most brutal inner battles. There is hope, and by allowing yourself the grace to accept your mental challenges, you can begin digging in, till, prepare, and nurture your soil for peace and tranquility.

TUNE IN TO TEND YOUR MENTAL HEALTH

Reflect on experiences where you have discovered a mental health challenge in your life or the lives of your family.

As you think about a crisis related to mental health, what have you learned from your experience?

How does knowledge of your ancestor's or relative's experiences inform the challenges you may undergo?

What have you found helps you weather mental health storms?

How have you become stronger because of someone else's vulnerability?

If you or someone you love is dealing with thoughts of suicide or severe mental health challenges, please seek help. Text 988 on your phone, or visit https://988lifeline.org

CHAPTER 10

Letting in the Light of Relationships to Cultivate not Hinder Growth

"There are two kinds of light — the glow that illuminates, and the glare that obscures."

—JAMES THURBER

As you contemplate harmony in your life's garden, think about how much sunshine plants require to survive and grow. However, too much direct sunshine can also deplete your garden and leave it burned and wilting. Your relationships can do the same.

Relationships can be the glow that illuminates your lives. Your friends and family tend to be where you find joy and fulfillment. As you raise your family and develop deeper friendships, you'll find that relationships are the light that helps you develop, grow, and find true meaning in your life. As you become in tune with those who matter the most to you, you remove those obscuring what is most important to you. Or you can stand back from those whose glare is stunting your growth. Living and growing in the light of great relationships requires continual care and intentional tending.

Relationships can trigger extremes of emotion—the greatest love, joy, happiness, and/or the deepest of pain, sorrow, and loss. There is always the risk that toxic goat relationships have blown your boundaries, people tromping all over your life, and not allowing anything else to grow.

Poor relationships can also stunt your growth. It is within your control, and you owe it to yourself, to identify which of your relationships will create long-term harmony. Though in the short-term, remember that most relationships go through the crests of harmony and troughs of discord. It may be challenging to think this way but understand that by putting your needs first, you can better care for others.

The possibility of being spread thin heightens without setting boundaries between your life purpose, vision, priorities, and your family's demands. I was speaking with a friend, Kara, whose husband had passed away. She turned toward her children, desperately trying to right the world turned upside down. Focusing for years on her children's growth and care due to the loss of their father, she had become lost to herself. Her center was no longer on her but on her children.

I asked, "What are your hobbies?" She could not answer the question, and it gave her pause, recognizing that she no longer knew who she was or what brought her joy.

Kara decided she needed to step back and get to know herself again. She took a part-time job getting out of the house and providing some distance from a never-ending flow of family challenges and responsibilities. It allowed her to network, connect, and find solace in her time at work. She created space and began to think about a future career, skills, and hobbies.

A common response to women investing time in themselves or their work is that they are perceived to neglect their "familial responsibilities," and Kara's experience was no different. She learned to ignore the negative slights and discovered that time spent at work or on herself didn't mean she was neglectful.

Instead, Kara found plenty of time to spend with her family after school and in the evenings, just as she had before. Now, her time was spent discovering her interests and investing in her personal and financial growth. She did this despite a family who felt women should not be working and was judgmental of her time out of the home. Ignoring her extended family's shortsighted ideas, she focused on herself first, allowing her to be more emotionally present for her children.

What is incredible about the shift in focus to yourself is that it resolves many work-life conflicts. When you have clarity on your purpose, vision and set priorities, it is much easier to have crucial conversations with those you love about what is important to you. Communication with family on your personal vision and how you can enable that for each other is how you find and create life-work enrichment.

Likewise, when discussing your vision and goals within the work environment, you must provide the same level of clarity to allow for life-work harmony. When working with my teams, I would hold weekly one-on-one meetings with my direct staff. It was the one thing I would not allow to drop from the schedule, and I would ask that each person bring a quick summary of their targets, what they had accomplished, and what they would be working on in the coming week. It allowed me to remove barriers and redirect as necessary to ensure they were working toward the right goals and vision for the team.

My job was to provide opportunities to develop skills and sponsor projects to help their development. In addition to weekly meetings, I would hold quarterly career development discussions. This was the individual's responsibility to bring forward their career plans. We discussed their longer-term goals and were required to spend time envisioning this future.

You can perform this same exercise with your family. Discuss finding purpose, defining a vision, and setting priorities. As an outcome, you will have clarity on how to support each other's vision. When conflicts arise, the discussions become more meaningful, and decisions become easier to make at the moment.

Decisions become streamlined with clarity in priorities when there is an opportunity for advancement, a trip that would take time from family, or a late-night project. Discuss which time or energy investments you are willing to make to achieve longer-term goals. Are the tasks coming from work aligned with your personal goals?

If not, you say, "No, this doesn't align," or "This doesn't work right now." If the opportunity aligns with your vision and priorities, you say, "Yes, more please!" or "For sure, I will take that promotion," or "Absolutely, I will take on that project that will extend my skill set and give me future career growth and financial success."

Let's be honest; not everyone has great support. It may be a challenge to discuss investing in your personal growth or asking your family to take on more domestic responsibilities so you can find time for yourself. It may be difficult to speak up about finances and not be faced with condescending or controlling responses. What I do know is that you cannot keep living a life where you minimize your personal goals for someone else.

Let me repeat: *Do not live a life where you minimize your vision for someone else.* You may alter your approach but do not stop the journey toward your life's vision.

LETTING IN THE LIGHT

You can choose who to invest time and energy in and give time to those who will enrich your life.

How do you get time for great relationships? You prioritize them. You review your time and identify who and when to fit in with those who will help you develop into the person you want to be. Those who tell you, "You are enough." "You've got this!"

"You can do whatever it is you set your mind to do. I am here to help you."

As a teenager, my son came to me in tears at the discussion of a friend who had been removed from his home because he was gay. Whenever I hear of a story of an LGTBQ+ son or daughter kicked to the street because they didn't match their family's belief system, my heart sinks, and my thoughts go out to them in love.

What if everyone followed the mantra, "Love and Accept All." Life would become much simpler, with no more judgment or toxic hate for those who are different or don't live as you think they should. You can accept your family's beliefs or practices, even if they do not align with yours, and you can always love them. Establishing yourself outside cultural norms without criticism or judgment when "love and accept all" is enacted. So many things in life and work would become more accessible as there would be no more active bias, tension, and no more fear of others.

Despite growing awareness, there are some relationships in which we must control the gates to our fences to ensure our psychological safety. I was having lunch with a mentored student, and over a hot bowl of soup, she paused and said, "My mom kicked me out of the house because I wouldn't do my brother's homework."

She had been raised in a family where the cultural norms were that men were more critical in having successful careers and that girls were meant to provide support. When she started failing to complete her homework and was putting her future at risk, she refused to continue doing it.

Instead of throwing judgment, I asked, "What would you do if this was not your family? What if this were your friend? What would you tell her?"

She said she would tell her never to allow it.

Hers was not an easy decision, and removing yourself from loved ones is always effortful. However, she knew she needed to be the center of her life and set firm fence lines. In response to her saying no to doing her brother's homework, her parents removed her from their home, and she moved in with a friend.

Sometimes you keep individuals in your life because of strong feelings, social expectations, or responsibility. However difficult it may be, setting personal boundaries with family, friends, and work colleagues is essential in finding inner harmony.

TUNING IN AND TURNING ON THE LIGHT OF RELATIONSHIPS

What relationships do you want to bloom?

What relationships exist only to consume?

Where do you feel harmony in your relationships?

What relationships do you wish existed, yet may still need to be developed?

Are you a Goat or a Gardener?

As you allow the light of great relationships into your garden, are you shining light into other gardens? Are you behaving like a goat or a gardener?

Becoming aware of your actions and how you may improve your interactions puts you on the path to becoming a master gardener, striving to become a haven for those you care about in a chaotic world. Take time to honestly evaluate if you are seeking to bloom or consume others. Below are some guidelines on how to become a gardener in others' lives.

GARDENERS LISTEN: When someone communicates their boundaries to you, listen carefully and try to understand their perspective. This can help you avoid crossing their boundaries in the future.

GARDENERS ASK FOR CLARIFICATION: If you are unsure about someone's boundaries, ask them for clarification. It's better to ask questions and be sure than to make assumptions and accidentally cross a boundary.

GARDENERS AVOID PRESSURING OTHERS: Respect others' right to say no and avoid pressuring them to do something that makes them uncomfortable.

GARDENERS RESPECTFULLY COMMUNICATE THEIR OWN BOUNDARIES: To create a relationship based on mutual respect, it is important to communicate your own boundaries and uphold them.

GARDENERS ARE OPEN TO COMPROMISE: Sometimes it's possible to find a compromise that respects both parties' boundaries. Be open to discussing different options and finding a solution that works for everyone.

GARDENERS RESPECT PRIVACY: Avoid prying into others' personal lives or sharing their private information without their consent. This includes gossip related to co-workers, friends, family, or your partner and perpetuates negativity.

GARDENERS APOLOGIZE AND MAKE AMENDS: If you accidentally cross someone's boundary, apologize and take steps to make things right. This helps to rebuild trust and shows that you are committed to respecting their boundaries in the future.

GARDENERS ARE AWARE OF THEIR BIASES AND ARE INTENTIONAL IN MAKING CHANGES: We all have bias, and it's okay. What is not okay is when we are aware and do not attempt to alter our behavior. Take time to become informed through training and doing the work to interrupt inappropriate comments, excluding others, inequitable decisions, or offensive actions.

Take time to consider your relationships and how you engage. Write your thoughts and possible gardening commitments below:

CHAPTER 11

Chuck It! Flip It! Use It!

"As a [woman] thinketh, so is [she]."

—JAMES ALLEN

Changing the outside world begins by changing your inner world. One primary insight you gain from life's experience is the understanding that the only thing you can control is your thoughts and reactions. You cannot control the whims of external forces that push and pull you into places you would never travel. Yet, going into uncharted territory builds resilience, and your ability to face any emotional demons builds necessary strength.

When planting a garden, you do not start by collecting your harvest; you begin by preparing, fertilizing, and caring for the soil you will eventually harvest. Understanding that your internal health is the soil in which all else grows, your prioritization of personal care ensures you grow the highest-producing life garden.

Recently, my father went through an extreme form of skin cancer resulting in the removal of his left ear, leading to a loss of hearing and a difficult journey to recovery. At the age of seventy-nine, he began daily radiation treatments, and through our two-hour trips to his appointments, we gained more time together than we had for years. As we journeyed from one side of Utah Lake to another, I shared the concepts I was exploring within this book, and he shared a simple story that has applicability as you prepare to plant your garden.

My father grew up on a small farm in Idaho, the oldest of eleven children; he was raised in a three-bedroom home. One room for the boys, one for the girls, and one for my grandparents and any new baby. As a youth, one of his first jobs was driving a tractor for Del Monte Foods. He would sit atop the tractor, driving and cutting the soil into rows, while four female co-workers sat on the back of the tractor feeding sprouts while a wheeled mechanism planted them in the lines behind.

He reflected, "What I found was most useful was to focus on the horizon, across the field to where we were going. If I happened to look to the side rows or behind me, the lines would always end up crooked. But it was always straight as an arrow when I stayed laser focused ahead of me."

You, too, can become sidetracked by looking to the side of you or behind you by looking at your neighbor, comparing yourself on social media, or doubting yourself by relating to a seemingly brighter student. Each comparison leaves you anxious and wondering why you are not as good or happy as everyone else. Looking behind you distracts you from where you are heading and leads to depression as you repeatedly look at your failures or decisions that resulted in what "could have been." To sow a straight line to inner health and planting for success, you must stay laser-focused forward on your journey.

Mental management is directly or indirectly tied to your *productivity, sustainability*, and *health*. Cultivating your mental well-being ensures that nutrients do not become deficient. As you tend to your inner thought processes, you place core nutrients required to nourish other areas, including relationships, work, finances, physical fitness, and personal development. The daily, sometimes hourly, fertilization of your mental soil occurs through reinforcing positive thinking and not letting toxic thoughts linger.

Ultimately, without the foundational work for good mental management, you see productivity loss at home and work and become burned out. You are looking for the energy necessary to focus on investments toward your vision. Your health may deteriorate as you cannot exercise, eat well, or find time for your fulfillment. Mental wellness reinforces all other aspects of your life; neglecting it puts it all to a detriment.

The premise of James Allen's work is that you are what you think. Your thoughts drive outcomes, and controlling your thoughts leads to positive success. It is easy to become trapped with toxic thoughts that erode the nutrients needed to see your vision come to life.

Rid your mind of negative thoughts and grow your harmony garden by opposing the "4 destroyers" – fear, doubt, shame, and guilt. Protect your mental health against these destroyers by creating boundaries with the outside world and, even more importantly, from your destructive thoughts.

CHUCK IT!

We all have negative thoughts; however, recognizing them and intentionally shifting them creates new thought patterns. Negative thoughts like, "I can't" or "I'm not qualified" paralyze your progress in fear. These thoughts keep you from planting healthy seeds, and weeds of doubt overgrow in your mind, leaving no room for positive outcomes. As you work on your vision and priorities, identify negative thoughts, and then "Pluck it! And chuck it!"

Plucking and chucking are easiest for those pesky thoughts that pop up out of nowhere, telling you, "You can't do it," "You are not strong enough," or "It will be too much work."

The list of thoughts and how they show up is never-ending. When you start to recognize the thought, you must interrupt it to get rid of it. It no longer needs to be part of your thinking; you must stop these thoughts before they grow and expand. If you have ever waited to weed your garden by allowing it to become overgrown, you know the importance of pulling them early.

One of the most memorable pesky weeds I allowed to grow was the internalized voice of my ex-husband telling me, "You are not a good mom." It took me years to realize this was his insecurity of not being a good parent and projecting his hurtful judgment onto me. It stayed in my mind playing like a repeating record player. Eventually, I took the time to pull that weed and chucked it in the damn garbage. Every time this thought weed pops up, it isn't as deeply rooted, and I pluck it and chuck it with well-practiced ease.

Some weeds are more challenging than others and can take extra time and effort, but the more you recognize the importance of plucking and chucking, the easier it becomes. As I shared this concept with one woman, she said, "I love this concept of *Chuck It!* but I think you need to replace the CH with an F. This resonates much more for me!" Hilarious, and if you are interested in using this format and it works best for you, please swap letters! What matters is that you are hyper-aware of your thoughts and not allowing negativity to take hold anywhere within your mental soil

FLIP IT!

"You are a wonderful mother," is my new, replanted thought. *Flip It!* removes and replaces the damaging weed with a positive thought. Most often, the exact opposite of what was said works. Similar to flipping a record from the B side to the A side, you shift your thoughts into ones that propel you into positivity.

The words "I can" create the most remarkable power statement, and utilizing them frequently puts your thoughts into super-powered action.

"I can't..." is replaced with "I can..." or "I won't..." is either "I will...." or "I don't want to."

For me to firmly plant the optimistic notion of being a good mother, it required that I wrote this affirmative statement down on a card and placed it next to my bed. Every night I would remind myself, "I am a good mother." No, wait, "I am an absolutely fabulous and freaking fantastic mother!"

The outside thoughts of so many others have been influencing your thoughts your whole life, and sometimes, they are so deeply embedded into your mental soil, that it takes a shovel, okay, maybe a track hoe to dig them up and replant. Over the years, I have had a series of these affirmative statements that I read nightly until I firmly believed them and created a new inner reality.

One of my biggest fears is the fear of financial ruin. Growing up without financial means and surviving extreme financial losses planted a deep-rooted thought that impacted my decisions. I had to take that fear of not being safe financially and replant it with the upbeat version, "You are financially safe."

There are so many weeds; they come from everywhere! Thoughts that tell you, "You are not good enough," "You are not strong enough," or "You do not belong."

All are massive goatsh*t! alerts and are ready to be flipped!

As I was working with our Tech-Moms Latinas group in 2021, one of the students raised her hand and said, "Is the tech industry even going to want us?" I looked around the room and could see everyone staring at me anxiously awaiting my answer.

My response was, "Who gives a shit if they want us. We are coming!" I then apologized to my co-founder Robbyn for my poor language. Everyone laughed, taking the negative pressure out of the room because we had now created space for a new positive mental path to be sewn ready for planting. For too many years, individuals have opted out of tech because they thought they would not be wanted or accepted. Their doubts and fear overtake them, not allowing that spark of a new vision for their life to become a reality.

Do not make decisions about your future based on the response of some illustrious make-believe "bro" out there telling everyone that you shouldn't come to get one of the best jobs out there because no one will want you. Stop this imagined person in you from telling you, "You don't deserve access to higher pay, flexibility, or remote working options to support your family because you don't belong."

It is time to *Flip it!* to positive statements such as:

* "I belong in tech. I am great at coding."
* "I love what I am doing and will kick ass in my new role."
* "People can't wait to hire me."
* "I have an amazing network of people that will connect me to incredible companies."
* "I am a badass mother who will successfully launch her tech career and have a fulfilling home life."
* "I am going to change the freaking world!"

All of that is so much more rewarding to say! (Even writing this felt good.)

Switching your mental thinking from questioning and fearful to more positive and affirmative thoughts will render successful outcomes. I have seen it time and time again. *Flip It!* works miracles as your inner thoughts begin to guide your outer presentation. Yes, it can be challenging if you are a woman in the workforce battling centuries of sexism—however, you should never allow the perceptions of others to derail you from where you are heading.

Flip it! Stay positive, look forward, and get aligned with your horizon.

USE IT!

Sometimes you can use challenges and negativity to your advantage. I drink dandelion tea as a detoxifier, helping with mental focus and immunity support. More often, we think of dandelion as a weed that is a disturbance in lawns everywhere. We pull them and scatter weed killer, giving us a luscious, green space. Yet, like dandelions, there are times when a negative situation and thoughts motivate you to create change in your life.

I was on my way to take my eBay team to a luncheon when I received the call from my doctor confirming a breast cancer diagnosis. I was driving on the highway, and nowhere to pull over. Somehow I made it to the next exit and the Thai restaurant where we were scheduled to meet. As I walked through the door, the bells over the door jingled, bringing me out of my thoughts to the present moment. I saw my team already seated, chatting casually across the room. I inhaled deeply, placed a smile on my face, and sat down, grateful that they continued their conversation so that I wouldn't have to speak.

I didn't tell my team about my diagnosis for a few more weeks. While waiting for my surgeon to provide more detail related to my biopsy, I continued going to work each day. I went through the days in a stressful fog, impacted by a lack of sleep and the real thought that I could die.

In addition to my father's current cancer battle, in 2018, he had also beaten prostate cancer. My mother survived uterine cancer; my grandmother passed away from breast cancer; aunts, uncles battled various forms of cancer; and my best friend/cousin passed away at thirty-eight from pancreatic cancer. The reality of my own cancer diagnosis set in and my emotions were deeply rooted, and there was no chucking or flipping the thoughts flooding my mind.

Once I won the battle with the insurance company, I began my battle with cancer and was scheduled for a double mastectomy. I informed my manager, and he responded, "Well, good luck." As a matter of emotional intelligence for any manager or human being, I highly suggest never telling anyone, "Good luck," when they inform you that they have cancer and will be in a fight for their life. Fortunately, the rest of my team responded more gracefully and quickly shifted to supporting all necessary tasks and projects while I paused work to focus on extending my life.

LEARNING TO LET GO

I was talking to a friend from the gym, nicknamed Cookie, and learned of the loss of his son to cancer, and realized the thought of losing a child to cancer was more shattering than the fear of losing my own life. My mind was reeling, I couldn't focus, and all was unclear. I would wake in complete panic, thinking I could be leaving my beautiful family.

Cookie suggested a book that became part of my daily life called, *Letting Go.*[6] I would listen to the text on the way to the office, learning how to recognize my emotions and not avoid them. I began to understand that I should not try to bury them because they would sprout elsewhere, negatively impacting other areas in my life. I became aware that you can use them to your advantage. Recognizing your emotions is a critical part of your humanity. Instead of pushing feelings down, acknowledge them, analyze them, and use them to create change.

I began to utilize the power of "letting go." In the weeks leading up to my surgery, I reviewed my life insurance, attended doctor visits, had MRIs, and grappled with my mortality. There were still tears; however, the extreme panic and anxiety somehow left as I set it safely aside. In a miraculous change in my mindset, I found a way to let go of the fear of losing my life. I realized

---

6   Hawkins, D.R. (2012). *Letting Go: The Pathway of Surrender.* Hay House.

that cancer was out of my control and holding onto fear was only ruining the life I had possibly remaining.

I was in a place where I was now moving through the journey instead of reacting to it, yet, I still had genuine emotional challenges. I allowed myself to feel the emotion, recognizing it was normal and that sadness and crying were okay. The most difficult thing I have ever done was sit down with eight children to tell them, "I have cancer." I cry as I write this as I recall the fear entering their faces, fading white, completely frozen in their seats, filling up our living room as I transposed fear into them. It was the worst moment I have ever experienced, instilling fear and potential pain in those I love most.

The room was quiet. Tears began to roll down a few of their cheeks, and everyone was looking at the ground. My husband Andrew explained why this might happen as best as he could. His intentions were in the best of places meaning to soften and relieve the burden they were all now carrying. He prompts, "Share your family's history with cancer," as if my family history somehow made anything better.

I did the best I could to explain what I knew and what I didn't know. "I will be having surgery and know more once it is completed." There was such limited information, and it felt like I was introducing more questions than I could answer. We finished with a prayer and a group hug, and nothing else mattered more than who was in that inner circle.

My youngest son, ten years old at the time, lifted the weight upon us as we finished our prayer. "Mom, I told you not to eat so much sugar!" The gravity of my message had not hit him as much as the others, and I was so grateful as we all broke into choked-up laughter. The kids dispersed, giving themselves space and the opportunity to handle their emotions in their way.

My stepdaughter remained, and my husband began to attempt to lighten things however he could. He began playing upbeat music, then shifting his tactic asking, "You want to go get some food?" I was completely spent and opted to take a moment alone lying in my bed, tears flowing as I attempted to recover from the heaviness and realness of the information I had finally shared, having carried it for weeks.

CRISIS-CRUSHING ARMIES OF POSITIVITY

Each day grew heavier until the day my husband called and said, "We would like to throw you a cancer party." What? This was the last thing I could think about doing. My mind was full of death and pain, thinking of my dad's and cousins suffering so recent and real in my mind. My first reaction was a definite "no." As the moments passed, I realized this might be a welcome shift and relief as I waited for surgery looming only a few weeks away.

My husband's business partner's wife became my party planning general, and my youngest sister her lieutenant as we assembled a massive Cancer Crushing Army of three hundred in less than two weeks. Friends, family, and individuals I had never met before showed up to give their positive thoughts of love and support.

The positive impact of that day is a gift that keeps giving. It is one of life's rarest gems, knowing you have a large army around you ready to activate at any moment in support. Thoughts of my army carried me through my MRIs, doctor's appointments, and surgeries, strengthening me through it all. If you are one in eight women diagnosed with breast cancer, parties filled with positive thoughts are what every warrior needs as they head into battle.

My outcome was positive. I could not say if shifting my mindset from fear to focusing on positivity allowed for a more successful outcome, but it did make my journey easier.

You too can *Use it!* Use your fear, doubts, shame, or guilt to create a more harmonious life. Seek opportunities to grow by abstracting challenges as an opportunity to reinforce your mental soil. Learn to "let go" and reframe your experiences from ones that were "forced on you" to ones where you are "the force."

Use it! Put your life's hardest experience into a positive force for growth.

TUNE IN TO YOUR THOUGHTS

Where can you utilize reframing methods to start tending to your mental soil?

CHUCK IT!

Remove toxic weeds of negativity, seek them early, and be intentional in what you allow to grow. Which thoughts will you remove?

FLIP IT!

Do you have negative thoughts you need to pluck, chuck, and replace? Which thoughts will you flip to the positive?

USE IT!

Self-motivate and identify opportunities that turn negativity into positive action. Which thoughts will you use to motivate you into action?

What are the most hostile and stubborn weeds, and which are the hardest to pull? (Remember, they will take extra time and effort, so be patient with yourself.)

CHAPTER 12
Pulling Weeds for Tranquility

"Life harmony is not to live without fear but to overcome your fear."

−TRINA CELESTE

Often, your most giant garden-destroying goat is you. Inner negative thoughts, hardened perceptions of yourself, and destructive self-talk will devour and destroy your mental energy. In a weakened state, the weeds of *fear*, *doubt*, *shame*, and *guilt* begin to sprout, taking over and making it impossible to sustain harmony. Feelings of depression and anxiety indicate that you need to set fencelines for your inner mindset and build mental reinforcements to thrive in all areas of your life.

Andrew Carnegie was one of the most visionary thinkers and influential people of the last century. In 1908, author Napolean Hill was commissioned by Carnegie and invested twenty years into researching how our thoughts lead to success. This research led to his book, *Think and Grow Rich*, published in 1937[7], which explores the power of positive thinking, goal setting, and perseverance as essential components for achieving financial success.

---

7   Hill, N. (1937). *Think and Grow Rich*. New York, NY: Ralston Society.

In one of their interviews, Hill and Carnegie discuss the relevance of societal systems for prisoners, but at one point, Carnegie shifts abruptly, stating,

> *"There are millions of people in an imaginary prison who have been charged with no crime. They are prisoners in their own minds, consigned there by their own self-imposed limitations."*

How many times have you felt like this? Stuck in the loop of negative thoughts you have built up around yourself, creating a mental prison cell.

To push through mental barriers, put yourself into purposeful action. You are propelled into action as you develop clarity about your purpose and vision for your life. Then, pairing your vision with strong mental reinforcements allows you to flip internal negative self-talk, disregard external negativity, sift through false statements, and use your experiences (good or bad) as opportunities for growth.

NURTURING YOUR MENTAL SOIL

Do you ever feel that you are a prisoner in your mind?

Where and how do you get imprisoned in negative thought cycles?

What thoughts imprison you? What thoughts make you feel free? Write a few of both below.

_____

_____

_____

What steps can you take to reinforce good self-talk? How can you reinforce thoughts that liberate you to take action?

_____

_____

_____

PULLING THE WEEDS OF FEAR

A few years ago, I was asked to speak at a local university on the topic of failure. I remember thinking, why would they ask me to speak on failure? Then I realized, oh yeah, it's because I'm really dang good at it! I am excellent at failure. I fail continuously, and I make mistakes every day. I make massive mistakes. I have hurt people, disrupted my family, lost businesses, and I still have massive fears of failing that I battle every day.

How did I learn to do this? You could say that I'm still learning. As they say, I'm building my wings on the way down. But how did I learn not to be so afraid of failing? I am no longer as fearful of failing, as the more times I fall, the easier it is to get up.

In college, I took a literature course on fictional writing. It was the only course in my college career where I had to engage a tutor. I had been struggling all semester and failed my mid-term final as I could not decipher and explain the concept of symbolism. My course load at the time included various math and computer science courses, and my brain could handle logic, numbers, and solid methodologies without issue. However, the vagueness of extracting an author's meaning by stating, "the curtains were blue," was beyond my comprehension. My thinking was the author was saying the curtains are blue because they are the color blue.

My professor was a short woman of Japanese descent, and her large black curled wig was teased to a frightening height in an attempt to bolster her size. I was absolutely terrified of her, as her grandiose teaching style would shift quickly into darting targets of fury.

During class, a student politely raised their hand and asked a simple question I don't recall. I will never forget her response, "Why do you ask such a dumb question?" The class of twenty all gasped, and our wide eyes darted to the "stupid student" waiting for a response, of which there was none.

One brave soul interjected the silence saying, "Ma'am, there are no dumb questions."

She said, "Yes, there is, and he just asked it."

I will never forget how we all immediately shut down with fear of ever asking another "stupid question" from that point on. I continued combatting my understanding of literature and its formalities, and I was on the verge of failing my mid-term and the entire course.

I sought help, and a petite and kind tutor saved my college career as her slight voice explained, "referring to blue curtains means that the author was inferring a state of depression and sadness." Ohhhh, okay... I finally got it and aced my final exam deriving symbolism all over that dang test.

This failure broadened my understanding of literature and my enjoyment of deciphering the meaning behind the literal words on the page. I find it ironic that I am now writing this book, and had I not learned from that failure, I may have never considered becoming an author myself.

Eleanor Roosevelt's famous quote, "Do something you fear every day," is burned into my psyche. I think of this phrase when I am afraid of having a critical conversation with my spouse, when I step into a new role I haven't done before, or when I decide to leave a financially lucrative position to start a non-profit. None of my success in life would have come without my ability to push past fear.

There are so many fears. Fear of others – what they say, how they may react, or fear of failure can stop you in your tracks. Sometimes you can even be afraid of being successful. I see this in my students as they say no to leadership positions or stretch assignments with the incorrect thinking, "If I get this job, then I am afraid I won't be able to care for my family." The fear of success limits their ability to care for their family more aptly.

My oldest son, Max, called me one day, standing outside the high school, "Mom, my anxiety is horrible. I can't open the doors to the school to go in." He had been dealing with severe anxiety for a couple of years and a deep fear that others were talking about or judging him would halt his ability to take any action. There were days when we would find him sitting in his car at the park next to the school, unable to drive home or to the school. This paralyzing feeling was becoming more and more pervasive and debilitating, halting his potential to graduate from school.

We pulled him from classes and placed him in a school with fewer students. He finished high school but not without impact, and his continued anxiety made it hard to connect easily with others. Then, one day at the age of eighteen, he said to me, "Mom, don't be mad." I remember thinking, *Oh no, who is she?* But then he said, "I enlisted in the Marines."

What!? First, why would I be mad? And second, how will this son who couldn't walk through the high school doors make it through Marine boot camp? How will he survive in a place full of strangers who not only talk bad about you but yell directly about how much of a failure you are to your face?

Deep down, Max must have felt that spark. My husky, blue-eyed, brown-haired son, whom I had nicknamed as a young child "My Rock," knew that he wanted to be a Marine and had to face all his biggest fears. Fears of not being enough, not being able to lose the thirty-five pounds it took to make it into the Marine Corps, fear of running every day, and fear of potentially failing out. I watched his journey while carrying my own fear and anxiety as a mother, watching him deal with the hardest of personalities, persevering through pain and disconnected loneliness.

Pushing through these fears came from within him, with purpose driving his resolve. Becoming a Marine wasn't one I would have ever prodded him toward; however, I recall him at the age of four running up the hill in his yellow rubber rain boots, always a weapon in hand, ready to conquer the world, and I see now it was always in him. He had dug deep and found his purpose, and WHY was pushing him beyond his most profound anxiety and fear and finally opening doors to a new broader world.

Your fear is nothing to be afraid of. When you experience deep fear, it's where you are going to gain the most growth. Failure is a critical part of your success and shifting mindsets from, "I am afraid, and therefore, I will not do" to "I am afraid, and therefore something absolutely amazing is waiting for me on the other side!"

This previous summer, I visited Max in Missouri as he graduated from his class, officially becoming a Marine and soon heading to Okinawa, Japan. We had a few hours of downtime, and wanting to get as much time together as possible, we found a place to park looking into the dark green woods surrounding the base. We then opened the car doors allowing the humid air and sunshine flow in while we chatted and filled in the gaps of lost time.

Sitting in the car, we reclined the seats back, and Max shared the latest songs from his Spotify list. I took stock of this refined and confident man as we listened to Barns Courtney's song

Glitter & Gold pump through the audio.[8] It was only a matter of months prior we had found him lying back in the seat of his car at a park, too anxious to go to school, and I was reminded just how much each of us has in us if we can step through the fear.

Life harmony is not to live without fear but to overcome your fear. Putting yourself at the center, tuning in, and recognizing your fears are levers in creating opportunistic growth. Take time to identify which fears may be holding you back from achieving your vision. As you conquer your fears, you reinforce courage and resilience, thus leading to growth and filling your life with harmony.

TUNING EARS AWAY FROM FEARS

What are your biggest fears?

Why do these fears exist?

What will happen in your life when you step through the fear and learn to let them go?

---

8   Courtney, B. (2015). *Glitter & Gold* [Recorded by Barns Courtney]. On The Dull Drums EP.

PULLING THE WEEDS OF DOUBT

When I entered college for my computer science degree, I had zero doubt. My weeds of doubt were planted after I started my college classes. Uncertainty was produced by professors questioning my ability, classmates excluding me, and my discomfort and isolation made me doubt myself and why I was there.

One day, a group project was assigned, and the group was all men and me. I had become shy, allowing them to lead the project while I sat back and watched. As they progressed in their plans, I began to wonder, *Why are they doing it that way? This is overly complicated. Am I stupid? Do I not have the skills that they have to be able to understand?*

The thoughts were running around and around, and then I just stopped, quietly half-raised my hand, and said, "Uh, what if we were to do it this way?" Their response was one I have never forgotten, "Yeah! That is better! Why didn't we think of that?"

What if I had kept my hand down? What if I hadn't said something? They would have gone off the deep end, and I realized then that *my voice matters*. I don't always get it right, but when I do speak up, more often than not, things go better. Throughout my career, not everyone in the workplace liked it when I was vocal and spoke up. I would get people saying, "You are too aggressive" or "You are too crisp." Well, I have ignored the ignorant people hundreds, maybe thousands of times, and I keep talking anyway.

As I entered my master's degree program, someone told me, "Trina, you are being selfish. You shouldn't go to grad school. You should be home with your boys." It was deeply hurtful and made me doubt myself and my vision to get my master's degree. I brushed it aside, and after completing my degree, I became the sole provider to my three sons. I had the fortunate circumstance of a more solid career because I pushed through the judgment and doubt and completed my degree.

STOP FEEDING THE WEEDS

Doubt is the destroyer of future success. If you let it take over, it will grow over your personal development and ability to scale in your career, limit your financial wealth, and impact your relationships. Doubt looms over you like those gargantuan weeds that cast a shadow over your thinking and tell you, "You are not enough." I am here to tell you, just pluck and pile those thoughts, get the red gas can, and incinerate those damn weeds to ashes.

You are enough, and there is a reason why those doubts become heavier when you begin working on something great. The number of books, training, and webinars on "imposter syndrome" shows that *everyone* feels doubt. Everyone. Imposter syndrome and doubt are not unique to women; everyone feels it. However, the difference and question you should ask yourself is, how much do you let it feed your weeds?

The risk in feeding mental time to our doubts/weeds is that it limits our potential and impact on the world. We owe it to ourselves, our families, our work, and our communities to remove our self-doubts and strive for our inner purpose. Take a time out and tune in to reflect on where you experience self-doubt and how removing it will further empower you in your journey to life-work harmony.

TUNING INTO REFUSING DOUBT

Where do you feel doubt? Do you "feed the weeds" by ruminating on your doubts?

How are your doubts limiting you? How can you propel your doubts into positive action?

PULLING THE WEEDS OF SHAME

TED speaker and author Brene Brown and the word shame are now synonymous. She has brought out the understanding of vulnerability and shame and how it limits us in our lives. Shame is one of the hardest and most emotionally triggering emotions for me. I have had to reinforce mental walls that look more like a bank vault than a yard fence—years of upbringing on the importance of a woman's morality and abashment of divorce, not once but twice, caused me to have deeply rooted thoughts and weeds of shame. Unfortunately, I listened to ignorant ideas, many from religious leadership, that pushed me into the cavernous depths of shame.

After my divorce, I was told several things I should have chucked but wrongly internalized.

"You will never be whole or happy unless you are married."

"You cannot reach God unless you are married."

"Your children are 63% more likely to be dysfunctional because you are divorced and single."

These statements are still burned into my memory. What I should have done was ignore and probably question their sources. However, I believed and quickly found myself in a second emotionally devastating marriage.

Shame haunts you, and it can prevent you from maturing and moving forward into healthy relationships as you limit yourself in fear of others' conjecture. I never allowed myself to detach from the shame, holding it tight. It was like a heavy anchor that held down my spirit. I had to release its grip and allow myself to sail freely towards self-acceptance and self-forgiveness, letting the winds of compassion guide me toward a brighter horizon.

The idea of sharing with anyone that I was married to a heroin addict triggered emotions of shame. Yet, when I discussed the writing of this book with my ex-husband, he said, "Using stories of shame is our way of making a positive impact." He has been in recovery for fourteen years, sponsored hundreds of others, and made his best attempts to be a present father.

He shared with me, "You know, had you not left, I would be dead." My sons have a father because I stopped the haunt of shame in my resolute statement, "It is time to leave."

Many of your life decisions are made to avoid shame, tip-toeing around the hurtful parts of your life in hopes that no one ever finds out, but they are ghosts that will always find you unless confronted. Cleanse your mind by challenging any negative thought patterns, beliefs, or behaviors associated with them. When ready, let others know of your pain, grief, and hardship, leading to healing, growth, and tranquility.

TUNING IN AND RISING ABOVE SHAME

What are you afraid others may find out about you?

Is there someone that you can confide in?

Are the weeds of shame holding you back in your life? What are they, and how can you pull them and clear your mind?

PULLING THE WEEDS OF GUILT

There is guilt, and then there is the goliath weed of MOM GUILT. It's an additional level of criticism that gets internalized and stops your growth. Mom's guilt arose for me from many places, like the neighbor saying with sympathy and a sad face, "Oh, I am sorry you *have* to work." I was thirty-five years old and had, at this point, been in my career for fifteen years, as well as a single mom of three sons. Her words burned with a not-so-subtle judgment of me not being in the box of society's role for moms to be in the home.

At first, this statement burned a hole in my thoughts, and hurt as I started planting her weed of guilt, *Oh, my life is so horrible. I never had a man to care for me and my children. I should always be home with my kids. I should not be building my career.* Then, a new thought sprouted up, allowing me to chuck the guilt and never let it grow again.

I paused, took a moment to tune in objectively, and inquired, *Wow, would I really be a better mom not having a career?* The answer was a definite *No.*

I reflected on all the great things I have done throughout my career and how knowledgeable I became because of my work. I traveled the world, understood different cultures, became an effective leader, and understood how to interact better and build others. I designed and developed software that positively impacted millions of users around the world.

The benefits of my career were not only to me, my company, and their customers but had a highly positive impact on my children. My sons understood what it was to work hard, not only as a man but as a woman. They benefited from my ability to provide financially. They respected the independence gained as I removed myself from difficult relationships. They knew how to study, and learned they can get through hard things.

During the founding of Tech-Moms, I would perform outreach daily to my network, asking for support, connections, and possible funding sources. One individual sent me a thank-you note for mentoring a friend's daughter while she was seeking her computer science degree, and I believed he would be a great supporter. He replied, "I cannot support your work for women in the workplace because I believe in family values." How is it that anyone would think that women working equates to not supporting family values?

In this case, I enacted an *ignore-the-ignorant people* stance and didn't reply.

There is too much guilt out there, too many ways we can get pushed into planting seeds of unnecessary sorrow. To pull the weeds of pressured mom guilt, it is vital to create awareness of the benefits of women in the workforce. This includes improved economies, higher corporate growth and profitability, and improvements in socio-economic impact. This awareness shifts the "mom guilt" mindset to empowerment, knowing that you are positively impacting the world by focusing on yourself and your skills and bringing your mind fully to the world.

A new positive mindset to battle mom guilt is embodying the statement, "I can have a fulfilling career AND successfully raise my family." In using AND, all things are possible, AND you decide how those two life aspects come together in harmony.

Remember this... No one should ever feel guilt for working. Ever.

Harmony cannot exist when you continually feel bad about developing yourself. Guilt for not being who others think you *should* be is a cheer swindler and the epitome of disharmony. Chuck it! And chuck it now! You are *exactly* who you are supposed to be and doing exactly what you need to do to find your version of harmony.

TUNING IN TO RELEASING GUILT

Do you ever feel guilty?

What triggers your feelings of guilt?

Is it coming from someone else? Who are the ignorant people that need to be ignored?

Is it coming from within? What weeds of guilt do you need to weed out?

CHAPTER 13

Becoming the Gatekeeper

"Family does not always come first."

–TRINA CELESTE

A poignant story was shared with me, illustrating the importance of becoming the gatekeeper of harmony in your life. It demonstrates that you may let cultural, societal, religious, or other expectations be the default gatekeepers of what you allow into your precious life. *Don't do this.* Learn from Laura in the story below.

I met Laura as she introduced herself to a group of students. She was bravely sharing a brief insight into her background and life challenges. She understood that by sharing her story, she might be able to inspire others and understand that they, too, are in control of their future and not at the mercy of their family or circumstances.

"I'd hit rock bottom and was not okay," Laura expressed these choking words as she wiped tears from her eyes while sharing a pivotal moment in her life. She explained that her "rise of the phoenix" moment came as a single parent living in a homeless shelter sitting with her two sons on her lap, eating dinner with strangers.

At the time, sharing a meal with strangers seemed an odd thing to be doing, as growing up, eating dinner together was something she had never done with her own family. But it was here that she began to build a new life, evaluate her relationships, and set clear boundaries. "I found friendships in the shelter, and they were genuine. There, I realized life is not all about family or community."

Laura spent years being raised in a family-centered culture that dictated that you do not put the older family members in nursing homes, everyone lives together, and you are not supposed to move out on your own. Expectations of Laura stemmed from cultural, religious, and societal expectations for a woman to care for others before herself.

"Our culture taught us to be codependent and that you should all work together, caring for whoever is most in need."

Laura explained, "I loved my mother, but I want to be open and real about the fact that she was diagnosed with bipolar disorder and was narcissistic." Laura's youth was filled with chaos, frequent moves, and a revolving door of relationships.

"My brothers were hard, angry boys, probably from their experience of instability and not having a role model or father figure in their lives." Even still, the pressure of cultural expectations assumed Laura would always care for her family. "I have been caring for myself and my brothers for a long time. It was just the norm, and I didn't know there was any other way."

Laura's mother had a boisterous and strong personality. She was highly entrepreneurial and started businesses where she enlisted friends, neighbors, and even her children. At age fourteen, Laura realized her mother had fallen behind in paying taxes.

"I remember the day the IRS came, making a count of everything. We had been living in a big house, and she was well-connected to some important people. She had been running various businesses and non-profits and ended up in jail."

GATEKEEPING: WHO IS IN CONTROL?

Before continuing Laura's story, I want to share a story with you about gates and gatekeepers. As a youth, my brothers and sisters loved playing with the goats we had on our small farm. We invented new games, one being "milk goat wars," where you would pick up a miniature goat and run around squirting your sibling with goat's milk. This was like a water gunfight. However, in our rush for fun, we would forget to shut the gates, letting them into the yard, resulting in senseless chaos with the goats destroying trees, flowers, and shrubs.

We watched firsthand how much goats voraciously consume when you neglect your gates. At an early age, I learned that we had to stay mindful and control the gates. We could let them in for fun and enjoyment and know when to keep them out to remain protected.

In Laura's life, she was at an age where she was learning what gates were and how to open and close them, and who to let in and out. But she was given extraordinary responsibility early in life, which she wasn't equipped to deal with. Even societal pressures wouldn't have dictated a seventeen-year-old to take custody of her four siblings, but her cultural expectations were so strong they became the primary gatekeeper.

TUNING INTO GATEKEEPING

Pause for a moment to reflect. Who do you make gatekeepers in your life?

As gatekeepers, do cultural or societal norms or expectations have your best interest at heart?

Consider the visual below. In each area of your life's garden, there are gates to which you control access.

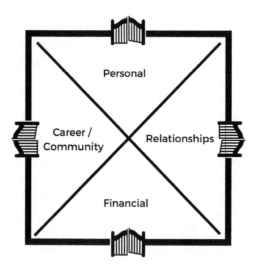

Controlling the gates

To find harmony in your relationships, you must become your gatekeeper. This is not a job you delegate to someone who doesn't know you, as often they would not have your best interests in mind. It's certainly not a job you can entrust to an institution or an abstract idea like a cultural expectation. It's also not a job to subcontract out. It's imperative that you determine who you let into your life and who you will you make sacrifices for.

LOSING YOURSELF IN THE SACRIFICE

Laura's parents divorced when she was two, and her father was not present in their life. "One day, I was driving past a park, and I saw him sitting on a bench, and he was homeless. It was wild." Although he was not present in her youth she has stayed in contact, and said, "He's been sober for nine years, and I'm grateful he's stable."

After Laura's mom was incarcerated, a request for early release was granted due to her having six months to live and young children at home. Laura's mother came home and lived with her children until her passing. Laura had assumed the role of caregiver to her brothers from the time her mother left for prison and continued after her passing.

Laura was sixteen years old at the time of her mom's death, and she gained custody of her younger brothers at seventeen. Laura was only a few years older than her eight, ten, twelve, and fourteen-year-old brothers and was still a minor. Her challenges were beyond what any adult could have been prepared to address.

But in a reassuring moment, Laura expressed, "I'm glad we're talking about mental illness. In my experience, we don't acknowledge that there's such a thing." Laura's struggles involved living a life impacted by mental illness. Not only her mother but her brothers exhibited mental health challenges. Her fourteen-year-old brother was found carjacking, had brought a gun to school, and was preparing to kill himself at school. "It was a cry for help."

Another brother entered a mental health facility after a bipolar diagnosis, and Laura would travel on weekends and sometimes two or three times a week to visit him. "I just didn't have the tools to help my brothers. The expectation was just not right. I could see they were going down and felt I had to pick it all up somehow. I assumed it would end miraculously, and I would then become happy. The truth is life is not always happy."

There are times when a family's expectations of you may be too high. You may be dealing with the mental or physical illness of family members, and the extreme pressure to handle others' care leaves you exhausted. You may be challenged by the high expectations placed on you through religious, cultural, or societal pressures. By default, if not controlled, external pressures become your gatekeepers. You risk becoming inundated with expectations to care for everyone else, leaving no space or remaining energy to care for yourself. As Laura aptly stated, "I got lost in my sacrifice."

RISING FROM RUIN

Now a single mom to two boys, Laura fell into even more challenging times as she and her sons' father split. She could not make ends meet on her own. Living in a culture where "family is first," she knew she needed a clean start to find herself first. In a life-altering decision, she moved into a women's shelter. She pivoted the trajectory of her life in this courageous step of saying no to staying in dysfunctional circumstances.

"My partner didn't know for two years that I had been living in a shelter while he was attending school." While Laura was at the shelter, she worked in a government position, and no one at work was aware she was homeless. Her work was strict on family and work separation, and despite having two young kids to care for and no home, she still received a promotion to supervisor. She received help with childcare support from her partner's family, but they were unaware of the harsh reality of her circumstances, and no one ever asked.

"I had to set boundaries of what I would and would not allow," Laura shared. Fence lines were placed and cemented, and she developed healthier friendships, enabling her to stay on course. She found strength in a new vision of what she wanted out of life. One where she centered on herself first, focused on what she wanted and what she could become, and where no one, including her children's father, her brothers, or her extended family—could push their demands on her any longer.

Over time, her partner understood what she required to raise their family. Together, they found help through counseling and attending finance and home ownership classes. They set goals and held to their shared priorities, and in time, their dedication allowed them to achieve their financial goals.

It has not been an effortless process, she said. "Many of my family members have become resentful and angry." But Laura held onto a new vision for herself, which did not allow her to propel her family's dysfunction forward. She had to say no, set boundaries, and disconnect from those who would derail her from her vision. As a reminder, the pressure never stops. You only become more attuned to what you want and block the goading goats' attempts to influence your decisions. Learn to expect it.

Stay centered on what is most important: yourself, your goals, and your future, which means you are not required to take in toxic family members. Put a stop to cultural or societal expectations that wish to dictate that and claim to know what is in your best interest. Understand, you will receive pushback when you are focusing on yourself.

Within two years of setting their new vision, Laura and her partner saved enough money to buy their first home. Her progress in such a brief time is tremendous and a testament to the power of focused attention to your purpose and vision.

I am grateful for that day when I asked if I could interview her and show her willingness to share her story and pour out her heart and soul. Her journey is beyond what many of us will ever be asked to endure, yet each of us have family or relationship challenges, both large and small, which can create a rift in our vision of our future selves.

You may have family members who love to nag, "You *should* be doing (this or that)," but deep down, you know it is not the right path for you. It may be a sibling, a spouse, a child, a parent, or a friend placing their expectations on how to act or behave. Understand that extending yourself too far due to family demands places your personal development and mental health at risk.

Until you are clear on your vision and priorities, your ability to have strong and courageous conversations with family or friends will be limited. Remember to set your fence lines and control who you will let in and who you will keep out. *Only invite in those who will help you bloom and keep out those who consume.*

CONTROLLING THE GATES EXERCISE

Time to tune into your relationships and adjust for orchestrated harmony. Whether it is removing a relationship or finding new relationships that help you grow.

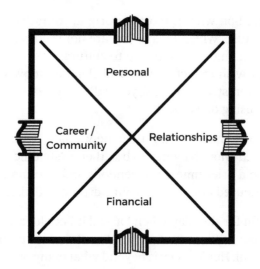

Controlling the gates

STEP 1: Draw your garden, put the names of those you love in it, and this will help you grow the inside of your garden.

STEP 2: List the names of those you need to set fence lines for, control the gates, and limit the time they get with you.

STEP 3: Lastly, are there any that need to be removed completely?

Visualizing your relationships this way will help you identify and prepare for conversations that will help you reinforce your fence lines and control your gates.

TUNING INTO YOUR RELATIONSHIPS

Who are the default gatekeepers in your life?

When feeling too busy, who are you allowing to control your gates?

Do you create the necessary time to build strong relationships?

Do you have friends or family you want to spend more time with?

Do you have friends or family that stop you from achieving your vision?

Do they draw energy or create an emotional burden?

Are you able to communicate your priorities to your friends and family members?

Are they supportive?

Do your friends and family enable and support you in finding time for your career, personal development, and financial wellness?

CHAPTER 14

Breathing the Fresh Air of Financial Wellness

"Financial freedom, is freedom from fear."

−ROBERT KIYOSAKI

Financial wellness is the air that allows us to thrive in all areas of life. Just like gardens need nutrients from the soil and carbon dioxide from the air to grow and give off oxygen, you will need the fresh air of financial wellness. As you plan for financial freedom, this will oxygenate every aspect of your life. In Maslow's hierarchy of needs, each level helps us develop upwards from the bottom. The needs are *physiological* (food and clothing), *safety* (job security), *love and belonging needs* (friendship), *esteem*, and *self-actualization*.

Maslows heirarchy of needs

Needs which are lower down in the hierarchy must be satisfied before individuals can attend to needs higher up. When we do not have the financial means to support our primary food, clothing, and shelter, we cannot expect to expand and invest in other areas of our life, leading to self-actualization and harmony.

I want you to see your financial future as an imperative part of your life harmony. I read Robert Kiyosaki and Shannon L. Lechter's book *Rich Dad, Poor Dad* during my early twenties, and created a vision within me to become a real estate mogul, or so I thought. If you are a female reader, replace this title with *Rich Mom, Poor Mom*.

I bought my first home at twenty-three while still in college. I was fully invested in my real estate dreams and plan. I read about investing, researched locations, and managed properties nights and weekends. I was living the bullshit epitome of "balancing it all." I was perceived as "doing it all" and "highly capable," however, I was not centered on my life vision and neglected myself in the process.

During these years, I decided to do my master's degree while performing bookkeeping for my exes' company, working full-time, and caring for my three sons, all in tandem. I ground myself down, attempting to fulfill my multiple visions and make everyone else's vision successful in parallel. In the evenings, you could find me traveling to homes handling rent, fixing properties, and prepping for new tenants, all with young children in tow, riding along in the back seat of my white Nissan Xterra.

We would learn new songs and play the "telephone game," where I would pretend I was calling them in the back seat, and they would answer, "Hello, who is this? How are you?" We would talk about the latest Power Ranger episode, bullies at school, or any new toy that had come onto the market. My life was so full I couldn't breathe, and at a later point, I realized I was spending too much time trying to build my husband's company and his success at my own expense.

For ten years, we did a variation of this routine. My boys grew out of the telephone game, and I spent a significant amount in my thirties building what I thought would be a solid financial future, only to lose much of my wealth in a matter of months. It is hard not to look back with regret knowing that had I held onto my real estate holdings, it would have generated tens of millions. However, the resiliency and education I gained during this time were not lost, and I have been able to rebuild into a new form of financial wellness. And along with that, I can now do it more reasonably, focusing on harmony instead of trying to balance everything. Because let's face it, working full-time, being a full-time mom, going to school, and running two businesses is the ultimate recipe for burnout.

Life often does not go as we expect. Once I became a single working mom, I recognized that managing eight rental properties and being a double-duty parent was not viable for my mental health. I had to prioritize myself, and my financial well-being took a temporary hit. But it did not ruin my vision of developing a solid financial circumstance for myself and my children.

RISE OF THE PHOENIX

Your most significant battles take place from the inside out. For me, there have been tangible battles: cancer, divorce, loss of financial assets, recessions, workplace setbacks, emotional abuse, and physical challenges. Yet, none of these ever were the real enemy; my largest enemy always came from within. It came from my emotions driven by thoughts that manifested physically and one day ultimately brought me to my knees.

It came suddenly as I walked into my bedroom one winter evening and could not stop the crushing force of stress, fear, and loneliness from converging. It landed with enormous weight on me until I found myself crouched over on the floor, my head almost touching the ground, and crossing my arms over my stomach in agony. I had experienced fear and loss before this, but at that moment, I was in absolute despair as I grappled with how to care for my three sons, ages seven, five, and six months old.

I was left with an extensive portfolio of nothing. After over a decade of developing my real estate investments, they suddenly dropped the bulk of their value in the 2008 recession. To make matters worse, I had invested fifty thousand dollars into a close friend's business, after which they filed for bankruptcy just two months later, taking most of my savings. I was alone with no one to provide for my family but me.

My tax bill that year was over one hundred thousand dollars as the losses on my homes were considered income, although I never saw a penny from the sales. My ex-husband was nowhere to be found, having taken off after giving him that check at Boondocks Fun Center. I was left holding all economic responsibility and tens of thousands of his debts.

I had no one I could go to as my family could not assist financially. All I had worked on, struggled, and sacrificed for was burning to the ground. I felt helpless as I watched it all be taken from me, with no way to stop the fire. The year was inundated with stories of extreme financial loss and I watched horrified as the news channels relayed stories of Wall Street brokers committing suicide, and several of my neighbors suddenly disappeared as they lost their homes during the recession.

As I walked into my room that day, the gravity of my personal and financial failure was so strong, it pulled me to the ground. I could no longer physically stand. I felt crushed by my fear of the unknown, my concern for my children, and how their lives would be altered. Overwhelmed by the weight of constant pressure and expectations, I found myself on the carpet, knees pressed down. It was like a vice grip clenched around my heart, threatening to wrench it from my chest. The physical agony mirrored the suffocating thoughts of a world closing in on me.

I sat in this state for only minutes, but it felt like hours, allowing all these intense emotions to move through me and surface as they expressed the seriousness of my financial situation. It was the beginning of what I have coined my *phoenix rising moment*, the pivotal shift where I would set the new vision of who I wanted to become.

I hung a framed quote on the wall in front of my bed that read, "You cannot go back and change the path from where you came, but you can change where your journey ends." I would read this every day as I woke up and each night as I fell asleep. I was determined to do something different and knew financial safety was integral to that vision. I was fanning the winds of change to blow fresh air into the airless pit of economic despair I had fallen into and to open windows into the rooms and corridors of my life that had suddenly had all the wind knocked out of them.

It was not a steady climb from the pit. The peaks and valleys were extreme, but I knew I could always move forward by taking ownership of my situation. Over the coming months and years, I rebuilt myself by putting together plans, setting budgets, and reading about healthy financial behaviors.

Slowly, the windows opened, bringing in a breath of relief as I saw the realistic future of financial security. I learned to poise myself like the Greek God Hermes, whose most remarkable feat was his ability to balance on the wind, allowing him to travel great distances easily. I had to strap on my winged sandals and take to the skies, controlling my response to life's winds as a force to stay aloft as I traveled the distance back to stability. I navigated life's challenges with improved grace and ease, staying on course to achieve my financial goals.

I had taken a new position at eBay and began setting aside savings. I created a long spreadsheet of debts, some my own and some left to me by my ex-husband. I worked from the smallest to largest (the debt snowball, as they call it) and celebrated each time a debt was paid in full. I began closing out the legal fees of my divorce, budgeting for childcare, keeping my mortgage and utilities paid, and working through the tax burden with my accountant in finalizing the losses of eight of my rental homes, letting go one by one.

Little by little, I found new moments of peace. I no longer ran around the valley checking on homes and instead focused on my children at baseball games and family dinners in the evenings. I took delight in the trivial things like my son eating his broccoli and laughing as he confessed it was hidden under the refrigerator. We made up rap songs and read together in my big white leather chair, all wrapped up on my lap, and I found moments of calm with my two boys and growing newborn.

I continued to excel in my work, receiving multiple promotions in a few years, allowing me the freedom to hire a full-time childcare worker and get out of debt completely. I was grateful I could hold onto my home and recognized that others could not do the same. As I pulled myself out of my previously despairing financial pit, I began opening windows of opportunities. I met my family's daily needs and refocused on the good within my life. I saw other areas of my life stabilizing, and I could breathe the fresh air of financial wellness once again.

BREATHING THE FRESH AIR OF FINANCIAL FREEDOM

You can find harmony when you take control and own your financial health. When you are not in control of your finances, you are not in control of your life or your family's future. As Kiyosaki says, "Financial freedom is your freedom from fear."[9] I would expand this idea that financial wellness leads you to find peace, independence, strength, determination, motivation, and power in all areas of your life.

This is because all aspects of life are tied to your financial wellness. Relationships, families, work, community engagement,

---

9   Kiyosaki, R. T., & Lechter, S. L. (1997). *Rich Dad Poor Dad*. New York, NY: Warner Books.

personal development, hobbies, living your purpose, and fulfilling your vision – all require money!

Growing up, I had incorrectly learned mindsets related to money. As the gardener of my life toward harmony, I had to pluck and chuck these weeds from my thoughts:

- ✗ Money is the root of all evil.
- ✗ As women, we should rely on our spouses to provide for us; a woman's job is to nurture.
- ✗ Someone else understands better than me how to manage my money.

All of these ideas were incorrect, and it took me decades and extensive financial losses to unlearn them and instead follow the corrected thinking:

- ✓ I am the best person to understand and make decisions about money.
- ✓ Securing financial wellness releases me from the grip of fear.
- ✓ Tending to my financial wellness allows me to achieve my personal goals.
- ✓ Being financially sound allows me to make a broader impact and change.
- ✓ When I am financially responsible, it provides me with the autonomy to make better decisions.

Your ability to own your financial wellness requires that you evaluate perceptions of yourself, belief systems, and mindsets that may be limiting your financial capacity toward life harmony.

Take time to pause and tune into limiting mindsets or behaviors that you may have toward money, working, or building financial wealth.

TUNING INTO IDEAS FOR FINANCIAL WELLBEING

Do you have negative perceptions regarding money?

What are they, and how do they limit you?

Do you avoid discussing or handling financial matters? Why do you think this is?

Do you have a sharp vision of your financial future? And do you have a road map of how to get there?

SETTING YOUR FINANCIAL GOALS

Remember, always start designing your life with you at the center. What is your vision for your financial future? Do you want to buy a house? A new car? Go on vacation?

Money allows you to care for yourself and those you care about. As you build wealth, you become financially independent, gain confidence in talking about money, and enjoy learning about financial markets and business. As a warning, too heavy of a focus on what we can obtain through money can mean we lose out on other aspects of financial harmony.

For years, I have consulted on business strategy (stick with me here), and when we start planning a business vision, I will counsel people to focus on two primary factors: *growth* and *profitability*. In your vision, consider how well you utilize your money to lead to personal growth and prosperity?

Money allows you to gain better healthcare, improve your relationships, and increase your knowledge, and all these combined gusts of fresh air lead to greater wealth. As you grow your wealth, windows of opportunities open. As you become confident in your choices, more options become available in your education, personal development, and career.

However, there is also a risk. As you begin to see financial growth, you risk becoming unprofitable. You do this when you spend unwisely, overutilize debt, and end up in the rat race again, chasing the next paycheck to keep up appearances.

To gain financial freedom, start with your life vision. You want to be building a profitable life. To do this, take control of your finances and set clear and obtainable goals. Be clear about how your finances will benefit you, which makes it easier to stick to your goals. Think about what it will be like to be financially free of debt, to be able to schedule a vacation, and to feel safe knowing that anytime a crisis comes, you are ready to respond financially.

Feel the breezes of freedom from debt, having ample savings to help you on a rainy day, and a plan for long-term wealth. You may have already accomplished some of the goals listed below. However, there is always more to learn when managing your finances. Open the windows and let in the fresh air of financial wellness.

TUNE IN TO 4 SIMPLE HIGH GROWTH & PERSONALLY PROFITABLE FINANCIAL GOALS

GOAL 1: Take ownership of your finances

GOAL 2: Create a budget

GOAL 3: Build a 6-month savings

GOAL 4: Invest in your long-term wealth

How will each of these goals support your life vision?

_____

_____

_____

_____

How will you feel once each of them is achieved?

_____

_____

_____

How much wealth do you seek to have, and by what date? (Be specific)

_____

_____

_____

_____

CHAPTER 15

Setting Fences for Financial Wellness

"Lack of boundaries, leads to lack of respect."

–ANONYMOUS

W e have discussed how financial freedom is the air that allows you to breathe life into other areas of your life. Yet, too often, you may give away your financial freedom to the "goats" of overspending, low aware-ness of how to build wealth, and pressure from others to allo-cate finances in ways not aligned with your vision. Remember that neglecting your finances leads to disharmony, and a lack of financial control contradicts achieving your vision.

Reinforcing your financial boundaries is foundational in finding life-work harmony. This requires a strong vision and commit-ment to prioritizing financial wellness through dedicated time and continual education. Jane Schwartzberg, head of client segments for UBS Wealth Management USA, said it well: "Eight out of ten women will end up alone and solely responsible for their financial well-being."[10] She continued, emphasizing how

10   UBS. (2018). UBS Own Your Worth report.
      Retrieved from https://www.ubs.com/content/dam/
      WealthManagementAmericas/documents/2018-37666-UBS-
      Own-Your-Worth-report-R32.pdf

problematic and short-sighted this is, "... we're not going to be prepared for what inevitably is going to come."

Not considering your long-term financial needs leads to a life of disharmony. On average, women spend ten years alone, and no one can afford not to understand and live the basics of wealth creation. According to the UBS survey, fifty-nine percent of the widows and divorcees surveyed regret not being more involved with financial decisions when married. Pay attention here, as *ninety-eight percent of those surveyed advised other women to take a more active role.*

This means everyone must take their financial wellness seriously. It cannot be ignored, as a renowned financial expert and author Suze Orman states, "A big part of financial freedom is having your heart and mind free from worry about the what ifs of life." [11]

Doesn't having a free heart and mind sound like harmony? Financial wellness creates the ability to not worry about whether you can pay that next bill, respond to that next crisis, or make decisions that are not dependent upon finances.

You may neglect your financial situation, as digging out of a financial pit can become emotionally overwhelming. But breaking it down into small steps to recover with a plan toward your life vision and then committing to it will get you on the path to financial wellness. Part of this recovery is reinforcing your fence lines and controlling your gates.

Research by Bank of America was conducted in 2022 on women and financial wellness. It found that ninety-four percent of women believed they would be personally responsible for their finances at some point in their adult life. Despite this, about half of women (forty-eight percent) felt confident about

---

11   Oprah.com. (2023). Financial freedom: Suze
      Orman's twelve steps to wealth. Oprah.
      Retrieved from https://www.oprah.com/money/
      financial-freedom-suze-ormans-twelve-steps-to-wealth-step

their finances, and only twenty-eight percent felt empowered to act.[12]

As you think about the goats preventing financial wellness, consider my childhood goats. In addition to consuming grass, shrubs, trees, and our vegetable garden, if left to their own devices, our family goats would eat any household remnants left out. Our goat Greta once ate my brother's muddy boots left by the back door. Garden hoses, plastic buckets, and even tin cans all fell prey to their trail of consumption. No item was safe, and they would be consumed if we were not paying attention. I would state that particularly proverbial pushy goats will eat your money if left lying around.

In addition to the goats of personal overspending, there are the ninny goats who ask for you to take on their financial responsibilities, and it occurs most often when you avoid these demon-eyed pillagers by shying away from talking about money. These life garden invaders will take over everything you try to bloom as they leave piles of their financial feces behind. Weeds of worry, doubts, shame, and fear begin taking over as you attempt to resolve newly introduced challenges. Now is the time to pluck and chuck the weeds, set your fence lines, and control the dang gates to protect your financial well-being.

As you go through this chapter, identify areas where you will regain control. As you do, you will find fulfillment in your financial growth and begin to breathe the air of financial prosperity into your life.

---

12 Bank of America. (2022, June). Bank of America Study Finds 94% of Women Believe They'll Be Personal Wealth Creators in the Next Generation. Retrieved from https://newsroom.bankofamerica.com/content/newsroom/press-releases/2022/06/bank-of-america-study-finds-94--of-women-believe-they-ll-be-pers. html

UNDERSTANDING YOUR FINANCIAL EMOTIONAL HEALTH

Financial abuse in marriage is more common than most are willing to admit or even realize it is a form of abuse. In many parts of North America and other world regions, women do not typically own their financial well-being. Yet statistics prove that women without financial freedom experience higher rates of domestic violence, including emotional and financial abuse. [13]

I recall a distressed call from a student the evening before her first class, saying she could not pay her tuition. "My husband and I got in a fight, and he took away my tuition money for class," she said. We worked with her to still attend, and she began taking steps toward owning her financial independence by gaining employable skills.

A study of women who suffered domestic violence by The Center for Financial Security found that ninety-nine percent also reported experiencing economic abuse, defined as "a partner taking control over a significant other's ability to acquire, use, and maintain economic resources." [14]

Let's take a moment to understand where you need to reinforce emotional fences related to money and put controls in place. You may be in a supportive situation or one where you are dealing with financial abuse. In either case, gaining financial control and understanding how money works for your benefit will bring confidence in your life's decisions.

13　National Institute of Justice. (n.d.). Economic distress and intimate partner violence. Retrieved from https://nij.ojp.gov/topics/articles/economic-distress-and-intimate-partner-violence

14　Center for Survivor Agency & Justice. (n.d.). Domestic Violence and Economic Well-Being Study. Retrieved from https://csaj.org/resource/domestic-violence-and-economic-well-being-study/

TUNE IN TO YOUR FINANCIAL EMOTIONS

Do you feel comfortable talking about financial matters?

If you are not comfortable, why not? How can you push through this discomfort?

Do you shy away from discussions related to money?

Do you feel stressed at the idea of looking at your financial situation?

If you are feeling discomfort, take a moment to pause and meditate. Envision how you will move yourself from discomfort to comfort. Think about opening a window, and white transparent curtains begin to sway in the breeze. Allow the thoughts of discomfort to flow out the window as the calm breeze of financial well-being flows in.

Now...

How can you improve your confidence related to money and finances?

_____

_____

_____

_____

What does financial success in your financial future look like, and how does that make you feel?

_____

_____

_____

_____

GIVING OTHERS POWER OVER YOUR FINANCES

Do not be deceived by financial analysts, educated business-people, family members, or friends—none of them will care for your money as well as you will.

For most of my life, I have invested in other' ideas instead of my own. I had this idea that everyone else knew more than I did and could create returns that I didn't know how to do. Uh, Goatsh*t alert! You *can* learn fiscal responsibility and invest just as much as anyone.

The two most powerful words in the English language are, "I can." Put yourself into intentional action and invest in yourself.

In 2020, as Covid exploded, I had two financial advisors, as that's what they called themselves, but I would now disagree. This is a very loose term for those handling other people's money. As the markets slid, one of my advisors panicked and sold most of my holdings without discussing with me. Their emotional state led to extremely poor decisions, and I lost a sizable portion of my funds. The other analyst was getting paid to use a financial system that everyone can access through a brokerage site like E*Trade, and I was paying them to do what I could do on my own.

I fired them both, took back what was left of my investments, and managed my financial investments independently. Each of our approaches to money is different, and that is okay. My husband and I have frequent conversations, reviews, and reallocations where needed. He wakes up at six am every morning and reviews stocks and investments for the first hour of the day. I am a once-a-month investment checker, as too frequent reviews of my finances trigger reactions that are not beneficial to my long-term plans. This investment approach helps me stay focused not on short-term gains but on long-term success.

Reinforcing boundaries exists not only with third-party financial analysts, friends, or family but within our mindsets. You find a truer form of harmony when you see your money put to work to build wealth and give you the freedom to achieve your life's goals. To find harmony, you must budget, save, and ignore the competitive game society pushes us into of always wanting a bigger house, a nicer car, and prettier clothes.

When I began building a non-profit, I had been in my corporate career for twenty-five years. For thirteen years, I was rebuilding from the 2008 recession. When the opportunity came to dedicate time to the Tech-Moms program, I could leave my corporate career and focus solely on helping women transition into more financially viable and flexible careers. I could not have launched Tech-Moms had I not been in a financially safe place. Caring for your finances gives you the means to live your dreams, whatever those may be for you.

Imagine your dream lies at the end of the rainbow. Look at financial wellness as the rain, which creates a rainbow guiding you to your vision. Your plan of economic health will be achieved in drips. Something as powerful as Niagara Falls is made up of billions of drops. Each drop is one small step you take towards financial freedom, and as the sun's light refracts, the showered drops enable your rainbow to emerge. Each small depth of thought put into action creates beautiful and powerful outcomes.

Step back, recenter, and realign your thinking to take hold of your financial power. Do you set aside the time required to learn how to build wealth? Do you allow others to manage your finances? How many economic decisions are you making? Do you have money of your own?

There are infinite resources available to anyone seeking them. You can attend webinars, and access to available classes on any form of financial education is only one Google search away. Be curious and learn how to create a budget, pay off debt, buy stocks, build a 401K retirement plan, and join financial investment education groups.

TUNING INTO YOUR FINANCIAL POWER

Do you have a financial wellness plan?

Do you own your financial decisions?

Do you continually seek to learn more about building financial wealth?

What do you think about your long-term retirement?

How would you now spend your money differently?

PUTTING MONEY IN YOUR OWN POCKET

As I mentioned earlier, in 2016, I had the opportunity to learn how The Global Hunger Project (THP) was helping tens of hundreds become self-reliant and overcome poverty and hunger. THP's core mission is to remove hunger from the world by 2030, and although this hasn't happened yet, they have made huge strides. One of their requirements for any community they work with is allowing women into all decision-making forums and creating micro-loans, which enable women to build businesses.

I recall a very astute comment by Cathy to a woman who had recently started a shoe-making business. She leaned in, lightly holding her by the upper arm, and said, "Make sure you put money in your own pocket."

In Cathy's experience of visiting hundreds of cities and villages in dozens of countries, she would see the same thing happening repeatedly. Women would earn the money and hand it all to their husbands. Losing control of how or where the money is spent, they could no longer participate in creating change within their communities.

Society becomes fully self-reliant once they have financially empowered women. A United Nations Clinton Global Initiative study found that women in developing countries invest up to ninety percent of their income back into their families and communities, compared to men who invest only thirty to forty percent.[15]

The study found that when women have control over household finances, they prioritize investments in healthcare, education, and nutrition for their families, positively impacting long-term community development. Your ability to make your own financial decisions changes not only your life but the lives of your loved ones and society.

Part of your financial success comes from your ability to earn an income. Recognize your power because you have so much to offer the world, and stepping through and owning your financial independence and knowledge will bring peace, calm, and confidence. In the coming chapters, we will focus more on the importance of "Watering Your Work Life" and how this, in turn, enables a more financially harmonious life.

BUDGETING YOUR TIME

Time is the one thing that is equally distributed for everyone; we each have twenty-four hours in a day. So, why do some of us have found financial success and others not? The answer lies in how we allocate our time. Time management applies to all four areas in our life garden (relationships, finances, work,

---

15   United Nations. (n.d.). Clinton Global Initiative. Retrieved from https://www.un.org/en/ecosoc/phlntrpy/notes/clinton.pdf

and personal development). Even the smallest amount of time reallocation to our financial wellness can be highly impactful.

You can receive significant benefits in small time allocations throughout the week when they are dedicated to reviewing your financial goals, researching, learning, and decision-making. I am not sure how many women spend time clipping coupons anymore, but I recall my mother trying to save a nickel here and a dime there by doing that. What if we rewind the clock and instead, she had invested the money in a few stocks forty-five years ago? The power of those few minutes could have had massive financial upswings for our family's future.

If you look at how wealth grows, it is through allowing it to grow on its own. I can't think of a better garden than one where you plant the seeds and then, as time goes by, the roots grow on their own! What if you could plant a dollar in the right place, and it would grow into $10? Would you do it? Well, you can! You didn't have to work for it; you just had to allocate time up front to ensure you were planted in the right places.

As you look at your weekly time allocation, find time to learn, research, and invest. There is immense power in understanding how financial markets work and how you can participate. It can occur in twenty minutes that provide substantial long-term benefits.

It may be the twenty minutes you don't look at TikTok and instead go to your budget and see what you need to work on. Then, spend twenty minutes less on domestic responsibilities and watch a video on investing in mutual funds, indexes, and stocks. (Laundry, dishes, or tidying up a disorderly house are a worthy trade.) Then, once a week, you find someone else to drive to a kid's event and take twenty minutes to use that time to invest $xx of your dollars into a new fund. Your reallocation of sixty minutes a week will lead to new levels of financial success.

You may be off social media or have different life demands than this example, however, there are areas where you can find even a few minutes to allocate to your financial health. Just like building muscle, it takes time to build knowledge and understanding. It may be painful as you watch markets rise and fall, but history has shown that the long-term investor wins, and it is best to start now. "No pain, no gain," as they say, and the pain as you plant your investment dollars today will increase your financial gains.

The lessons and joy you will find in owning your financial well-being are something no one can do for you or take from you. When a crisis hits, divorce, health, or job loss, you know you are okay and have the tools to rebuild faster. So, let's hit the financial gym and build that money muscle!

TUNE IN TO REINFORCED FINANCIAL WELLNESS

Your path to financial wellness and the harmony which flows from it begins with you. Let's take time to recenter and tune into the next steps you will take in reinforcing fence lines and finding financial wellness within your life.

FINANCIAL HARMONY CHECKLIST

- ☐ Chuck it! Remove negative emotions related to money.
- ☐ Set clear and obtainable financial goals.
- ☐ Set financial boundaries for yourself by saving and budgeting.
- ☐ Don't give your money away; own your financial power.
- ☐ Seek financially viable careers and promotions and strive for higher income.
- ☐ Network with others who have similar goals. Create or join an investment club.
- ☐ Learn continually through podcasts, eLearning, websites, and classes.

- ☐ Mentally prepare for financial difficulties. Don't quit, and don't ignore.
- ☐ Use your time wisely and allocate regular times to review your finances.

PERSONALIZE YOUR CHECKLIST

Take the checklist above and create your own set of financial guidelines below:

☐ _____

☐ _____

☐ _____

☐ _____

☐ _____

☐ _____

☐ _____

☐ _____

☐ _____

☐ _____

☐ _____

☐ _____

CHAPTER 16

Tapping Into the Wellspring of Work

"Stop watering things that were never meant to grow in your life. Water what works; what is good; and what is right [for you]."

–UNKNOWN

As I have led various women's organizations through the decades, individuals would bring up a hesitation to move up in their careers because they said it would "derail them from their families."

A study conducted by the American Psychological Association in 2010 found that the children of working mothers tend to have higher academic achievement and better social skills compared to children of stay-at-home mothers.[16] The New York Times notes that children whose mothers worked when they were young had no major learning, behavior or social problems, and tended to be high achievers in school and have less depression

---

16   American Psychological Association. (2020). The role of gratitude in buffering the negative impact of economic stress on psychological well-being [PDF file]. Retrieved from http://www.apa.org/pubs/journals/releases/bul-136-6-915.pdf

and anxiety." [17] If you are worried about a career and kids, there is no reason you cannot change your mindset from one where you "have to work" to one where you "get to work."

In 2015, a preliminary study by Harvard Business School Professor Kathleen McGinn, who works as a Cahners-Rabb Professor of Business Administration, research of women whose mothers stayed home full-time found that women raised by an employed mother are twenty-one percent more likely to be employed, twenty-nine percent more likely to supervise others at work and earn more money. [18]

The full study published in 2018 identified working mothers' sons were more egalitarian, had a higher rate of working wives, and shared a higher load of domestic responsibilities and care for their children. This study found no difference in children's "happiness" levels between working and nonworking parents.

"People still have this belief that when moms are employed, it's somehow detrimental to their children," says McGinn. "So, our finding that maternal employment doesn't affect kids' happiness in adulthood is really important."

Your work choices should not be based on raising happier kids. McGinn continues, "When women choose to work, it is a financial and personal choice. Women should choose based on whether they want or need to work, not on whether they are harming their children—because they are not."

Sheryl Sandberg's book, *Lean In*, corrects perceptions of what it means to be a working mother, including that higher pay

---

17 Miller, C. C. (2015, May 16). Mounting evidence of some advantages for children of working mothers. The New York Times. Retrieved from https://www.nytimes.com/2015/05/17/upshot/mounting-evidence-of-some-advantages-for-children-of-working-mothers.html

18 Harvard Business School. (2015, September 28). Kids of working moms grow into happy adults. Retrieved from https://hbswk.hbs.edu/item/kids-of-working-moms-grow-into-happy-adults

means more options and a higher likelihood of achieving our vision and harmony.[19] You can hire a childcare worker, a gardener, or a house cleaner. You can get help and stop trying to "balance it all," and learn to focus only on those things that are most important to you. It is time to chuck the guilt and believe financial wellness provides greater opportunity for your children than being with them 24/7. Center your mindset on quality time rather than quantity.

As discussed in a previous chapter, it's important not to make cultural, religious, or societal expectations your default gatekeepers. When you do this, you may lose motivation and risk burning yourself out for the dreams of someone or something else who doesn't have your best interests at heart.

As you water your career, your skills grow, your financial wellness grows, your relationships expand, and you develop personally and professionally. Having additional discretionary money means that you can better assist your family and be a stronger financial provider. Pew Research Center states, "The share of women who earn as much as or significantly more than their husband has roughly tripled over the past 50 years." Twenty-nine percent make an equivalent amount of money, and sixteen percent of wives are the primary breadwinners.[20]

If you are the breadwinner, great, if you are not the breadwinner, great. Who the primary or secondary provider is does not matter. What matters is your financial independence and the power this gives you to make intentional decisions about your life. Working is an enabler that allows you to put yourself back in the center of your life.

---

19   Sandberg, S. (2013). *Lean In: Women, Work, and the Will to Lead.* Alfred A. Knopf.

20   Pew Research Center. (2023, April 13). In a growing share of U.S. marriages, husbands and wives earn about the same. Retrieved from https://www.pewresearch.org/social-trends/2023/04/13/in-a-growing-share-of-u-s-marriages-husbands-and-wives-earn-about-the-same/

No one should hold themselves back from earning higher incomes or building their careers. Yet, I see women limiting their career growth for many reasons. Women are being pressured to quit, limit their income to part-time, take lower-paying positions incorrectly deemed "family-friendly," and not push themselves to higher-paying jobs because they believe this would prevent them from caring for others. (Quadruple goatsh*t alert!) The truth is a higher income increases your ability to care for yourself and those in your care.

THE WELLSPRING OF SELF-SUFFICIENCY

Throughout my thirty-year career working with thousands of women, I have heard their stories and felt their fear, angst, and emotion as they transform their lives from co-dependence to independence. One of these closely affected me was a story from Anna, a single mom of two autistic daughters. She had been a supportive wife, always willing to give, support, and enable the entrepreneurial endeavors of her husband. It was a situation that looked like a perfect scenario on the exterior, as one where she was "taken care of."

Last year, I started the TikTok channel @trina.celeste. Because I talk "tech" and "moms," the TikTok algorithms began serving up videos of moms jumping around on couches and drinking wine in the middle of the day, expressing how great their life was because they did not have to work. The harmful fad of the #momtok crowd highlights the way the world pressures women to find value in the fact that they are not working, and it is taking a massive economic and emotional toll on women.

I have heard this belief from youth as well. When taking a group of young girls to a STEM conference for the first time, I asked, "Do you know what STEM stands for?" One girl replied, "Yes, science, technology, engineering, and math. But I am not good at math."

My heart skipped a beat as I inquired, "Why would you say that?"

Her follow-up response stopped my heart altogether, "It doesn't matter. I am going to be just like my mom and *sleep all day and shop all night*." The way she sang like a tune, I knew she was mimicking an anthem of codependence. One that was harming her and her future. It is a misguided message to our youth that they are not responsible for their financial welfare.

Lack of financial independence is one of the leading reasons one-third of the world's women cannot find emotional and physical safety. Estimates published by The World Health Organization (WHO) in 2021 indicate that about one in three women worldwide have been subjected to physical and sexual intimate partner violence or non-partner sexual violence in their lifetime.[21] Within Anna's household, emotional, financial, and domestic violence was the norm. The fear of being alone and unable to provide for her daughters kept her in a harmful situation for too long. It was a situation where financial control would be used to coerce into sexual and financial abuse.

As the level of violence increased, Anna was finally faced with a considerably larger fear than fear for herself as she witnessed her spouse's actions impacting her daughters. Her daughters gave her the courage to leave, yet the anger and control escalated in parallel to her strength as she placed personal boundaries to protect herself.

Her unwillingness to be controlled by anger or threats led to an incident where, when picking up their daughters, she and her spouse argued while she was standing outside his car. In a rage, he shifted the car into reverse, hitting her. Their daughters watched from the back seat as he drove away, leaving her injured behind them. She would find out later she had a broken hip requiring a total hip replacement.

No one else had seen the incident except her daughters, who could not testify due to their autism. Anna held her head high

21 World Health Organization. (2021, March 9). Violence against women. Retrieved from https://www.who.int/news-room/fact-sheets/detail/violence-against-women

and exemplified the strong mother she knew her daughters needed. Mentally, emotionally, financially, and physically broken, she began the hard road of rebuilding her life from the ground up.

Anna connected with a state-sponsored program for women experiencing poverty, found Tech-Moms, and enrolled. Throughout the program, her eyes opened to the career opportunities available. She began to see herself accomplishing much more than she had ever dreamed. She dug in and learned how to code in the evenings, on weekends, and between appointments for her daughters, who required continual care.

She began to see where her life could go and applied for a full-ride coding scholarship, beating out five-hundred other applicants, and just over a year later became a certified web developer. Her challenges in managing her children's needs and recovering from her trauma required continual effort in orchestrating harmony.

As she rebuilt her life, she knew she could no longer neglect work. Her future harmony depended upon finding a career that would sustain her and provide her with the flexibility necessary when caring for special needs children.

Anna's vision of creating a different life for herself and her daughters inspired her, and she found gratification and purpose through connections in the tech community. She began giving back to others experiencing similar situations as she joined as a Tech-Moms Teaching Assistant, enabling others to find personal power in their career development and skills. Setting aside windows of uninterrupted "me time" allowed Anna to focus on developing her career skills and accomplishing her future vision of moving into a full-time role as a web developer and getting off state financial dependence.

Career journeys are never easy, but they're rewarding in finding financial independence, fulfillment in your work, and discovering that you have much to offer the world. Looking at work as a part of your life instead of something that "has to be done" allows you to *take back control and determine what you want to do in life instead of life being done to you.*

TUNING INTO YOUR CAREER MOTIVATIONS

Do you hesitate to work? Why?

What are the fears, doubts, or outside pressures that are preventing you from developing your career?

How can you address any of these limitations to build a stronger career?

CHAPTER 17

Watering Your Work Aspirations and Channeling Your Fierceness

"Women belong in all places where decisions are being made. It shouldn't be that women are the exception."

–RUTH BADER GINSBURG

One of the largest prohibitions for women in building a career is simply a need for more awareness. Growing up, you may not have seen women in successful corporate careers, and educators are not typically equipped to provide visibility into all the existing opportunities. This lack of awareness is harmful, as a study published in the *Frontiers of Psychology* in 2017 found that exposure to counterstereotypical female role models early in development can increase women's motivation to pursue challenging roles.[22]

---

22 Olsson, M., & Martiny, S. E. (2017). *Does Exposure to Counterstereotypical Role Models Influence Girls' and Women's Gender Stereotypes and Career Choices? A Review of Social Psychological Research.* Frontiers in Psychology, 9. https://doi.org/10.3389/fpsyg.2018.02264

You cannot be what you cannot see, and to create the greatest success in your work life, you need to step beyond and discover what is available. Growing up, my brothers and I would watch the movie, *Conan the Destroyer*. Arnold Schwarzenegger and his muscles enthralled my brothers, but for me, Grace Jones as Zula was the freaking bomb! It was my first time seeing a strong FIERCE woman, and I wanted to exemplify her.

Throughout my life, I have often asked myself, "How would Grace handle this?" The reply, "She would tackle it with fierceness! Raahhh!" My inner voice can be quite intimidating.

Start tackling your work life with fierceness! The beginning step is understanding opportunities and roles that will work for you. Within the Tech-Moms program, we bring in industry experts that discuss their roles, how they got there, how much they are making, and how the participants in our program can move into these careers. So often, we hear, "I just didn't even know this was an opportunity for me!" The visibility spurs into active decisions with clarity in available pathways. Career transitions are further excelled by knowing others who have paved the way to success.

Remember the "commit and shift" discussed in Chapter 7? Find and attack a path, and then shift when ready. Selecting or transitioning into a career can be daunting, and fear of making the wrong decision halts many in their movement forward. Understand that *there are no wrong choices*. The only wrong choice is to do nothing at all. Any education, experience, and time working builds additional skills that will translate as you shift throughout your career.

A frequent response to career exploration is, "I recognize there are so many options. I want to do this, and this, and this..." Pick one. Don't be wishy-washy; remember, there is power in decisive actions. Then ask yourself, how would Grace Jones (or your own empowering role model) do it? She would grab it and act! Once you commit to a single career path, you will experience that opportunities arise. Your conversations become clear as you can relate, "Here is what I would like to do," and then follow up with the question, "Do you know how I can get into this role?" You will be surprised how confidence in your next steps and talking without hesitation enables others to help you get there.

In order to find a career that works for you, return to your purpose and vision, and ask questions to those in roles that will help guide your next career step. Schedule time with individuals and conduct informational interviews, asking, "What is your role?" "What is a day in your life like?" "What do you like about what you do?" "What do you not like about what you do?" "What drew you to this career?" "How did you get into your role, and what education did it require?"

In doing these types of interviews, you are doing two things:

1) Learning about various roles and getting exposure to opportunities.

2) Expand your network of contacts as you can then go to them when job searching.

Both are ways of spending time and giving your work aspirations plenty of water, which you can draw from throughout your career. Informational interviewing works as you enter a new career but can be used as you explore new opportunities throughout your career.

THE RISK OF UNDERWATERING YOUR WORK LIFE

Orchestrating harmony requires constant navigation, and it is possible to underwater or overwater your career. Have you ever felt stuck in your role, unable to find the next step, or afraid to move forward? Caught in the trap of, "Well, I'm comfortable and will just keep doing what I am doing." Underwatering your career is a disservice to yourself.

Growth occurs when we become uncomfortable, yet many stay stuck because we do not identify as someone who should move to the next level. A Harvard Business Review article identified two ways you could expand your career: first, internalizing a leadership identity, and second, developing your sense of purpose.[23]

Purpose: You cannot discount the power of this in developing your career. Using the purpose you created in early chapters, you can align it to the opportunities within a company. You will find more energy, authenticity, and drive for your work when you align your career with your life's purpose.

One student, Sheila, was outgoing and loved to connect and build relationships. She loved technology but felt torn because she had to choose between using her technical skills and her people skills. As she networked and met with others throughout the tech industry at events and meetups, she discovered a perfect role aligned with her purpose of connecting with others to solve problems, and she became a technical sales engineer.

Sitting back and staying "as is" will be insufficient to meet your life's needs and may derail you from finding harmony by settling for careers that minimize your inherent abilities. There is a career fit out there for you which aligns with your life purpose. One that will bring you energy and excitement and amplify your ambitions. Do not fall into drought by underwatering your career. You have so much to offer the world, and when you do not put yourself into positions of impact, you are taking away something extraordinary the world needs.

You must look past the status quo to see what is possible and identify your compelling reason to act despite personal fears and insecurities. You can take the time to align your sense of purpose by pursuing career goals that align with your values.

---

23 Hagel III, J., & Singer, M. (2014). From Purpose to Impact. Harvard Business Review. Retrieved from https://hbr. org/2014/05/from-purpose-to-impact

In doing so, you advance the collective good of those in your inner circle and make a broader impact.

TUNING INTO WORK ASPIRATIONS

How can you align your purpose with your career?

If unsure about your career, how can you take steps to discover opportunities?

STEPS TO WATERING YOUR WORK ASPIRATIONS

ENVISION YOUR CAREER

◆ Always be focused on the next promotion or position for higher income. What is that next role for you? How will you get there? Who can help you get there?

WARNING: *Do not stay where you are because you are comfortable. Discomfort brings growth, and growth brings income, personal fulfillment, and a positive life impact.*

PUT YOURSELF OUT THERE

- Attend networking events and connect with others who have similar jobs and goals.

- Expand your network beyond your friendships. Find others to learn together and connect to new jobs and opportunities. This is critical for continual career development.

DEVELOP YOUR CAREER SKILLS

- Get involved in social networks and join or start groups focusing on developing similar careers.

- Read books, podcasts, and increase your knowledge.

MENTALLY PREPARE FOR EMOTIONAL DIFFICULTIES

- Do not quit; resiliency is a life skill that you are developing.

- Acknowledge that careers are not a straight line; you may jump up, down, and shift sideways with an understanding that it is all additive.

- Learn from your mistakes. Correct them and move forward quickly toward the future.

- Know it will be emotional, and that is okay.

OWN YOUR FINANCIAL HEALTH

- Develop courage and understanding of potential bias in hiring. Ask where your pay sits in proportion to others in the same role.

- You can discuss your pay with others in the same role to ensure it is equitable.

- When interviewing, come in prepared for industry-standard pay for a similar role. Then ask for their pay range.

WARNING: *Do not mention your prior pay, if you share that your pay was lower, it sets you up for a lower pay scale immediately. The best option is not to provide prior pay and instead ask for the pay range for the role.*

Everyone will be in a different place in their career. Start with where you are, and do not compare yourself to others. As a helpful reminder, refer to Teddy Roosevelt's quote, "Comparison is the thief of joy." Stay focused and centered on your career path and goals, then identify the steps to move toward your vision of success.

A goal is only a wish unless you write them down. Take a few moments to write down your goals in achieving your ideal career.

CHAPTER 18

"Opting In" to Career Power

"The wisest decision in life is to embrace opportunities as they arise, for without doing so, both your life and the world as a whole may stagnate or diminish."

–TRINA CELESTE

L ife-work harmony often begins after a forced reality check. You might be pushed into challenging circumstances like losing a job, a spouse's illness, or loss of work. Life's unplanned circumstances can set you outside your comfort zone, requiring you to look for a job, find a higher-paying career, or one with more flexibility. Many women we work with are leaving jobs like nursing and teaching due to low pay, difficult hours, and non-negotiable life demands. Ironically, the jobs society deems "acceptable for women" are often the WORST jobs for moms.

The Tech-Moms mantra is, *Tech Jobs are Mom Jobs!* The reality is that every job is now a tech job, and opting to gain these employable skills enables every career. Thousands of women are transitioning to careers where flexibility, remote working, and higher pay are available. There is an increased awareness of technical roles and understanding that they provide well, often enabling life-first-work harmony.

It is essential for women to see themselves in economically viable, higher-paying positions that also offer flexibility for life-work harmony. Part of the requisite awakening is removing incorrect thinking, which assumes who belongs and who doesn't belong, and the belief that "women can't do this work."

Everyone belongs! There is room enough for everyone in any life-enabling industry, there is a role fit for everyone, and most importantly, you *can* quickly learn and develop your skills.

The common phrases of, "I'm not good at math" or "I'm horrible at tech" are self-limiting and keep you from accessing incredible opportunities and building necessary skills for the future. These beliefs limit your children as you cannot share ideas and options that would expand their future. You are opting out of helping to create a better future for all of society.

Create a long-term commitment to your career path, as more women and mothers are needed in the industry. When you opt in instead of out there is a massive long-term economic and social impact, and generations behind you are influenced by your decisions and actions. Whatever your career of choice is, take it seriously and make it a priority.

In 2019, I was working as the global president of eBay's Women in IT organization, and we were hosting an event in San Jose in partnership with an organization called GLAM (Girls Leadership Academy Meetup). Through a two-day conference, girls ages eight through twelve were introduced to business management, marketing, product development, and technology skills. They were placed in groups and asked to innovate ideas, learn how to develop them into a business model, put together product outlines, and define marketing strategies. They then presented their proposed company's pitching on stage to three hundred employees and family members.

Executive female judges from some of Silicon Valley's most prominent companies came to provide support and feedback to these young girls, many of whom came from challenging family scenarios and foster care. Seeing the girls' excitement was inspiring as they dug into their creativity and were open to learning all they could as they designed their businesses. It made me ask this question: *When is it that women begin to opt out?* If these girls were so eager to dig in and develop their skills, when is it that we begin to say, "No, I can't."

As we finalized and listened to each group present, one of the business pitches caught me off guard. A girl with long brown hair in a hot pink tutu hovering over her striped leggings said, "Our mobile application is for all those alone in the hospital and want to connect to others. We want no one to feel alone. Finding other patients who may be going through what they are going through will help them heal faster."

These brilliant minds did not realize I had just been one of those patients. I had undergone a bilateral mastectomy a few months prior. There was a moment after surgery, as I lay in bed in pain, when I thought: *I heard there were two other women who went through my surgery today; I wonder how they are doing?*

These insightful minds were years ahead in their thinking. But I'm concerned these impactful ideas and the voices behind them are forever going to be muffled. At that conference, I recognized millions of ideas have been glossed over simply because women are opting out, ideas that could potentially solve the world's largest and most complex problems.

What if, as women, we stopped opting out? What if you could put all your ideas into action through education and under-standing how businesses and technology enable the opportu-nity for change? To do this, you must reinforce the importance of work and education for yourself. You are opting into your power.

ESCAPING THE "YES" TRAP, AND THE POWER OF THE PAUSE

You each have a unique gift that can be grown, developed, and used in beneficial ways. However, it is so easy to get distracted and derailed by the goats surrounding all sides of your fences. You may have a goat boss who has overrun your work schedule, leaving you feeling depleted. You may have family demands that continually interfere with your work, like a sick child, housework, elder care, shopping, and/or community involvement, which overtakes your ability to stay focused.

Taking control and reinforcing your fence lines across all areas ensures you orchestrate harmony as you go. You must be clear about your goals and *say yes* to the most important things. My husband quotes John D. Rockefeller to me frequently, who said, "Don't be afraid to give up the good to go for the great."

Do you know what is good versus what is great in your life? When you're unclear, you will find it challenging to decipher. You will fall into the "yes trap" as a default response to everything. As I've been authoring this book over the last eighteen months, I've had to practice saying no, focusing instead on prioritizing those things that bring me harmony. Completing this work has done just that, and I knew it would get done, however there were multiple times when I had to pause and say, "Not now," to other tasks.

When Tech-Moms began to scale, I paused writing so that we could accomplish something greater. My greatest goal was to see that dozens of classes were successfully launched, business operations were in place, allowing us to scale, and that each of our student's outcomes and experiences was exceptional.

Having a dedicated focus on the vision of scaling our non-profit business meant I had to shift away from my personal goals temporarily. As a result, we received sufficient funding to support hiring a team (all prior Tech-Moms), providing the bandwidth necessary to shift back to my personal and business goals.

Had I attempted to do all these good things simultaneously, I would not have been able to do anything remarkable, and in 2022 Tech-Moms was recognized as Utah's Non-Profit of the Year by the Salt Lake Chamber. The recognition was a testament to a shared passion and focused on coming together to provide a platform to expand our reach through visibility, partnerships, and access to funding. Remember, this is where harmony comes in. We must tune in to see what feels uncoordinated. We must listen and act, ensuring what is being asked of us will lead us to the vision we have orchestrated for our lives.

Remember my junior high band teacher that I mentioned in chapter 2, Mr. Boone? He performed miracles with a class of unruly teenagers by pausing and tuning in. He listened for harmony, and so must we. Hold up that conductor's baton in your own life, and do not let anyone tell you when you're ready for the symphony to start. *You're in charge of orchestrating your life.*

Taking time to tune into your goals, and prioritizing them, allows you to orchestrate each moment. Taking temporary intentional pauses and redirecting allows for ebbs and flows between your priorities.

TUNING INTO DISCERN CAREER PRIORITIES

Take a moment to list your career goals. Nothing is off limits, list everything that is most important to you as you develop and build your career. Once done, take a moment to prioritize this list. Are there any that seem promising but a "not now" and others that may be great, "Yes, let's get freaking going!"?

Yes, I am ready to rock!

_____

_____

_____

No, not now

_____

_____

_____

CHAPTER 19

Conducting Self-Advocacy in Your Career

"Place yourself in the conductor seat of your career, not your manager."

—TRINA CELESTE

As you tune into your career, conversations with your managers will improve. Communicating your career vision enables your manager to assist you in skill development, provide stretch assignments, and assign roles as they become available. Having clarity in your goals and communicating them helps your manager or a sponsor within the organization identify potential growth opportunities. Remember, *you are in the conductor seat of your career, not your manager.*

Not every manager understands or empathizes with the life experiences of those they lead. You must take responsibility for your career development, ensuring that conversations occur to help bridge awareness. Carve out time to discuss your personal development goals and how you can tie them to corporate goals.

For example, if your company is making a big pivot into artificial intelligence (AI), you could ask if there is an opportunity to engage in related projects. At the same time, you study AI in your spare time. You could ask if they would sponsor classes for you to attend and ask what opportunities they may see coming and in which areas.

Conversations like this assist in a few ways. First, they show your manager you're seeking growth opportunities enabling them to pull you into stretch assignments. Second, it creates broader connections and relationships with your manager, and third, it will allow you to have conversations about the goals and expectations, which lead to higher potential in promotion opportunities.

Do not shy away from career development conversations at any stage of life. I have seen students in their fifties, sixties, and even at the prime age of seventy-seven transition their careers. It does not matter where you are; come prepared to discuss your vision and purpose and convey how you can be of value to the company.

REINFORCING CAREER BOUNDARIES THROUGH COMMUNICATION

As you discuss your value at work, be clear about your work hours, availability, and things like responding to emails after hours. For many years, I would work eight to ten hours a day, then do another two hours in the evening, prepping for the next day's workload. This was unsustainable, and I learned the importance of guarding my home time as sacred.

Having crucial conversations related to work hours allows for understanding and adherence to your boundaries. In my experience, when I had conversations around my work goals and understood my expected results, I could say no to unnecessary tasks and meetings and stay focused on those things, which enabled my career development.

Do not tiptoe around about the fact that you have a life outside of work. For many years, I held back talking about being a parent in my workplace because I felt it would be met with bias from some who I imagine thought things like: *She could not handle leading an international team, raising three exceptional sons, and five remarkable step-kids.*

Well, I was wrong in holding back. Instead of "hiding" my life circumstance, I could have been open and discussed it productively. As I became more open, it allowed for awareness and led to solutions that enabled life-work harmony. It had a secondary effect, as my team felt more comfortable speaking about their life and conversing with me on how we could address temporary life interruptions and orchestrate harmony in the office.

I would use humor to explain, "Yes, I have three sons and five step-kids." To diffuse their predictable response, I would joke, "If you add them up, it's like twenty-seven kids. Plus... two nannies, and an orphaned cat named Fluffy." My attempt at math humor interrupts the shock of having a large family, builds rapport, and at times minimizes the judgmental question of whether I can truly do it all. I found ways to confront and convey that I was capable of much more than biases may have allowed. In tackling potential biases upfront, I began to expedite my career AND continued raising a fabulous family.

DON'T BE A GOAT!

When I say, "Don't be a goat," I am not talking about being the *Greatest of All Time! Those overly focused solely on their greatness typically are not the greatest*—I am talking about not being pushy and consuming invaders on others. Stay focused on your goals, present your value, and how you benefit the company.

As a caution, frequently bringing up your personal life challenges is unnecessary. However, dedicated conversations in your career development and life coordination with your manager should be taking place for you. Conversations on life-work priorities and openly discussing how to coordinate your preferences when temporary life disruptions arise will allow you to partner on how to address your needs best.

To overcome any fear of these life-work conversations, come prepared with "Here is what I understand are my work priorities, do you agree?" and then follow up with, "Here is how I see I can meet these and handle my priorities as well, do you agree?" Come with a solution proposal and how you see what you can address.

As you speak up and share your life responsibilities, be concise and understand that you should not overshare. Take caution as you share, reinforce your boundaries, and ensure you respect others. Dumping all your dirt and spilling out all your current trauma and challenges puts an unwelcome burden on your manager. In these cases, you have become the goat, placing your emotional weight on others around you. You don't want to be the goat.

If you're new to a position, sometimes it's nice to get your feet wet before you begin these conversations. You may be thinking right now, *there's no way I can discuss my home life with my boss, nor do I think my manager will support discussing long-term career goals.* Still, if this thought persists, you should reevaluate your choice of employment, especially if you're unable to discuss promotions and career trajectories with the person who is paid to help you succeed in the workplace.

Dealing with a boss who won't support your career can be a challenging and frustrating experience. Unfortunately, some managers do not accept their role in your success. Here are some steps you can take to address the situation:

COMMUNICATE: The first step is communicating with your boss about your career goals and the support you need to achieve them. Be clear and specific about what you want and ask for their help in achieving your goals. If your boss is not receptive or dismissive, consider sharing your concerns with a trusted colleague, mentor, or HR (Human Resources) representative.

FIND MENTORS AND SPONSORS: Look for mentors or sponsors within the organization who can offer guidance, active support, and advocacy. This person can be a senior leader or someone who has successfully navigated similar challenges and is in a position of influence.

SEEK OPPORTUNITIES: Look for opportunities to develop your skills and gain experience outside your current role. Attending industry events, networking with colleagues, and taking on challenging projects will help you build your skills and reputation.

DOCUMENT YOUR ACHIEVEMENTS: Keep track of your accomplishments and successes and highlight them during performance evaluations and discussions about career progression. Agree with your manager on the frequency of sending regular status updates.

CONSIDER YOUR OPTIONS: If you have exhausted all options for addressing the situation with your boss and are still not receiving the support you need, you may need to consider other options. Start exploring other job opportunities, either within your current organization or outside of it.

You should always be actively engaged in career exploration and identify your next three steps. This forward-looking approach sets the vision and helps you create clarity in each step toward achieving long-term success.

Considering your career's next three steps is essential as you take control of your professional growth. By thinking ahead and identifying your next steps, you can align your actions with your long-term goals and aspirations. When you have an unobstructed vision, it becomes easier to make strategic decisions regarding your career. You can evaluate various options, such as job opportunities, training programs, or skill development initiatives, based on how they contribute to your long-term goals. This ensures that your choices align with your desired direction and enhance your professional development.

Mapping out your next three steps provides clarity and direction in your career journey. This clarity and direction can increase confidence and focus in pursuing your career goals.

It helps you set milestones and benchmarks, which can serve as motivational indicators of progress. Having a clear plan also enables you to communicate your aspirations effectively, whether it's discussing career growth with your manager, networking with professionals in your field, or seeking mentorship.

Lastly, continuously considering your next three steps, you create a forward-thinking mindset that fosters continuous learning, growth, and adaptability. This approach positions you for long-term success by staying ahead of industry trends, acquiring new skills, and embracing opportunities that align with your evolving goals. It lets you remain proactive in shaping your career path and adjusting when needed.

Remember that career planning is not a rigid but a dynamic and iterative process. Your next three steps may change as you gain new experiences, encounter unexpected opportunities, or reassess your priorities. Regularly reviewing and adjusting your plans ensures you remain agile and adaptable in navigating your career journey.

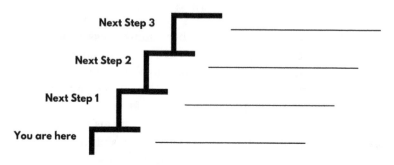

Three steps ahead

Remember, you deserve a supportive and encouraging work environment that allows you to reach your full potential. Do not be afraid to advocate for yourself and seek opportunities to help you achieve your career goals.

REMOVING OFFICE HOUSEWORK

There is office housework, and then there is the home house-work. Both can derail you from life harmony quickly. Trivial things add up to hours of lost time and focus. At home, you may get caught up in the laundry, cooking, cleaning, running errands, and a million other non-essential tasks. In the office, these are typically the non-value-added items, including sched-uling meetings, preparing events, running employee activities, or hosting an office party. They sometimes must be done, but sometimes they do not.

Orchestrating in the moment what is a priority and must be done, and what can wait is an essential life-work harmony skill. Ask yourself, "What truly needs to be done by me, and what can be delegated or shared?"

Too often, we say yes to non-essential tasks, and I have heard, "Well, it's just easier to do it myself." But, to achieve life-work harmony, you must share the load. Conversations at work on priorities allow you to determine what is critical and what is potential housework. Ask yourself, "How does this align with my performance goals?"

Burnout is a multifactorial syndrome caused by factors related to the work environment, workload, job demands, lack of con-trol, and limited support. You risk disharmony when you're not focusing on your priorities and instead are responding to a never-ending task list of non-essentials, quickly becoming overwhelmed and burned out.

World Economic Forum's research report in 2021 shows that women who are asked to perform extra levels of office house-work, such as the emotional labor of cultural improvement ini-tiatives for diversity, equity & inclusion, taking notes in meet-ings, organizing social events, and random managerial process improvements go unrecognized and unrewarded. Social expectations of women to handle low-priority tasks must be mitigated, as those taking on these additional activities report higher levels of burnout and lower job satisfaction.[24]

Stay tuned into the level of exhaustion at work. To battle the risk of burnout, stay focused on your career development, become hyper-mindful of how tasks are distributed, and ensure you perform tasks aligned with your core job responsibilities. Be aware of office tasks you are performing that are not part of your job description, but you do them anyway because they are needed. Here are steps you can take to stop doing them:

CLARIFY YOUR JOB RESPONSIBILITIES: Clearly understand your job duties and responsibilities. Focus on tasks essential to your role and avoid taking on unnecessary charges.

SET YOUR FENCE LINES: Be clear about what you can and cannot do. If someone asks you to do something not part of your job, politely decline and explain that you focus on your core responsibilities.

DELEGATE TASKS: If you have team members or colleagues better suited for certain tasks, delegate those tasks to them. Focus on your core responsibilities and help others develop their skills.

COMMUNICATE WITH YOUR MANAGER: If you are consistently being asked to do tasks not part of your job, speak to your manager. Explain the situation, and request guidance on how to prioritize your responsibilities.

SAY NO: It is important to be comfortable saying no to requests not part of your job. It can be challenging, but it is essential to prioritize your time and energy on the tasks that are most important for your role.

---

24 World Economic Forum. (2021, November 16). Women in the Workplace 2021: The invisible labor holding women back. World Economic Forum. Retrieved from https://www.weforum.org/agenda/2021/11/women-workplace-2021-invisible-labour/

HANDLING HOME HOUSEWORK

In addition to reinforcing time boundaries at work, look at other areas that may consume too much of your time and prevent your growth in all areas of your life.

When my husband and I merged families, I felt a strong urge to embody the role of Martha Stewart, or the more recent homemaking celebrity Joanna Gaines, taking on the responsibilities of cooking, cleaning, and tidying to create the perfect home. However, my attempts at cooking were far from successful, leading to what we now fondly refer to as the "Dirt Fish Incident," when my culinary creations tasted less than appetizing. As I hurriedly dashed around, striving to bring order to the chaos, my husband observed my actions and asked, "What are you working on? I wish you would sit down; you seem frenetic."

At that moment, something clicked within me. I realized that constantly rushing and not letting myself slow down created more tension than I was resolving. It was a revelation. I became aware of the frenetic energy I was radiating and consciously decided to pause, sit, and take a deep breath. I understood that everything could wait, and through the practice of mindfulness, I began to interrupt my autopilot mode and reassess my true priorities.

I discovered newfound clarity by embracing moments of stillness and redirecting my focus. I learned to identify what truly mattered in the grand scheme of things and let go of the unnecessary frenzy that had consumed me. This shift allowed me to approach my blended family life with a greater sense of presence, intention, and peace.

In that moment of reflection, I realized that creating a harmonious home wasn't about striving for perfection or juggling a multitude of tasks simultaneously. It was about finding moments of peace, practicing self-care, and recognizing that true tranquility comes from within.

Shortly after, my husband received an accolade as CEO of the Year, presented by Utah Business. The days leading up to the event were a whirlwind of responsibilities at home and work. Amidst the chaos, household chores took a backseat, resulting in a daunting pile of dishes in the sink. We coordinated with friends and extended family the morning of the event, ensuring that our eight children were prepared for the ceremony.

The awards ceremony was an unforgettable occasion. We were overwhelmed by the support and love shown by so many, and we cherished every moment spent with our family. As we returned home, a lasting image etched itself into my memory. Without uttering a word, my husband walked through the door, removed his tie and suit jacket, rolled up the sleeves of his white collared shirt, and began tackling the mountain of dishes. Here stood a man who could have been out celebrating with fellow executives, yet he chose to celebrate with soap and suds, accompanied by the energetic beats of Depeche Mode.

I am incredibly fortunate to have a partner who understands that traditional gender roles do not determine housework responsibilities. He recognizes that everyone must contribute their fair share in managing the daily demands of life. While you may not have someone to roll up their sleeves alongside you, you can determine your priorities and what and when you will allocate time. It is not about having someone physically present to share the load but embracing the mindset that household responsibilities should be distributed by mutual agreement, not gender.

When looking at your home life, reinforce boundaries around your time and create space for your relationships, career, and space for yourself. Here are some strategies to limit housework and orchestrate life-work harmony:

PRIORITIZE AND DELEGATE: Make a list of the most important tasks you must accomplish both at work and at home. Identify the most urgent and vital, and delegate other tasks to family members. Free up time and energy to focus on the most important tasks, and do not feel you must finish all tasks every day!

SET FENCE LINES: Establish clear boundaries between work and home. Set specific times for work and stick to them as much as possible. Similarly, designate time for personal and family activities and avoid scheduling work-related tasks.

USE TECHNOLOGY AND AUTOMATION: Use technology and automation to streamline tasks and save time. For example, use scheduling tools to plan meetings and appointments, use a grocery ordering app to schedule your food delivery, or utilize prepared meals services that will free up time for you.

SIMPLIFY YOUR ROUTINES: Simplify your daily routines to save time and energy. For example, plan and prepare meals in advance or use a shared cleaning schedule for your family to participate in and spread-out household chores over the week.

TAKE BREAKS / PUT YOURSELF IN "TIME OUT": Take regular breaks throughout the day to recharge and refocus. Use mindfulness practices to recenter and tune in, even briefly, to help you renew and recharge. This practice helps reduce stress and improve productivity.

Remember, it is impossible to achieve work-life balance. Instead, you must pause and tune in, continually orchestrating life-work harmony. It is about limiting housework, setting realistic goals, managing stress, and prioritizing self-care. By proactively managing your time and energy, you are creating a more fulfilling and harmonious life.

TUNING INTO CAREER PRIORITIES

Take a few minutes to be proactive in next week's activities. Set aside time at least once a week to decipher what can be dropped and what is a priority.

Then again, each morning, identify which activities are the highest priority and then do a "delete or delegate." Each time you review, you are opening space for harmony to flow!

CHAPTER 20

Creating Space for Growth & Transformation

"If a [woman] achieves victory over [herself], who in the world can exercise power over [her]? [She] who rules [herself] rules over the whole world."

–VINOBA BHAVE

As you continue growing an exceptional life garden, you must create space for yourself to grow personally. Creating space for personal development helps you become more self-aware, grow as an individual, overcome obstacles, and improve relationships with others. Not taking time for self-reflection or personal development will lead to burnout and a lack of fulfillment in your personal life.

At the age of forty, I began to experience extreme pain in my lower back. The pain would radiate down my legs with increasing intensity over time. I got to the point where I was unable to lean over to pick up items off the floor. Often, I would find my back buckling and crash to the floor next to what I was trying to retrieve. My husband and I had recently married, and using my nickname, he jokingly expressed his concern, "Beenie, I don't think our prenup has a clause for back issues, but hey, we will tackle this one vertebra at a time." A solid attempt at lightening humor, but my pain wasn't so funny, and I was deeply concerned.

I had gone to several doctors and chiropractors over the previous year, attempting to manage the pain. Fortunately, I made it to a doctor who x-rayed my lower back and confirmed my concern by telling me, "You have level three of four degenerative disc disease. You basically have the back of a 60-year-old."

What? I am forty and way too young to be dealing with this! I thought.

My fear of surgery and long-term health impacts woke me up. I began researching fitness approaches to handling back issues and increased my time at the gym.

One day, I unexpectedly asked a woman in her fifties with a stellar physique, "Do you happen to do fitness training?" Fortunately, her answer was yes, her name was Jill, and she had been a National Figure and Bodybuilding competitor during her forties. I asked if I could build her website in trade for fitness training, and she agreed, and our work together was pivotal as I began creating additional space for my health.

Looking at my schedule, I ensured my fitness was always at the top of my daily list, and my meal planning was done weekly. At the time, I was working full-time and mothering a new family of eight children, but even so, by being intentional about putting myself at the top of my life's priority list, I always managed to find the time.

Waking most days from 4:30 to 5:00 a.m., I would do my workouts, then visit Jill to go through my nutritional plans, set goals, and track progress. Fitness became a hobby that would yield benefits later as I fought for my life.

For the next two years, I learned to be intentional in my workouts and how much diet impacts everything. I refined my eating habits, adjusting them for travel, daily life, and work. It became part of who I was.

Each workout reduced my lower back pain and also benefited my mental well-being. My energy increased, and my client engagements were smoother whenever I started with a solid day at the gym. It became noticeable to my kids, as any day I was abrupt with them, they would ask, "Mom, did you not work out today?" We would laugh because they would often be correct, as I had missed my morning mood-stabilizing session!

In time, I saw changes. New muscles would emerge, and my strength would increase. I loved learning new workouts and dug into building my physique in ways I did not understand before. I stopped doing endless cardio and focused on proper nutrition and weightlifting.

Within a year, I began getting requests for photo shoots for fitness advertising. This was not in my wheelhouse or an area I would have considered, but then I thought, "Why not become a fitness model at the age of forty-two?" Watch out Grace Jones! I was on my way to becoming my version of Zula, except with a family of kids in tow and a high-pressure corporate position.

But in 2019, I was diagnosed with breast cancer. I was in the prime of life. This shift to prioritizing my personal development gave me five years without the severe pain I experienced prior. Yet, I was fighting for my life in this new health crisis. I had no symptoms, and I felt great, but even so, I entered the battleground. It was here I learned that your daily actions cannot always prevent life's challenges; however, they do help you get through.

After going through bilateral mastectomy surgery and coming through the recovery, my surgeon commented that my recovery was one of the fastest she had seen. I was shocked as they work with hundreds of women a year. But looking back, had I not dug into finding ways I could manage my lower back issues, I may have had a different outcome as I went through cancer.

The daily routines and habits you create have a long-term impact on every aspect of your life. Whether improving your health and wellness, increasing your knowledge, expanding friendships, or developing new hobbies, finding space for yourself will benefit every other area.

Your ability to feel harmony depends on finding space to develop and grow. As you increase your health, intellect, and connection with yourself, you become more energized, happier, stronger, and more confident.

There are five areas of personal development.

1) **PHYSICAL HEALTH AND FITNESS:** Practicing healthy habits, like exercise and proper nutrition, to maintain physical well-being.

2) **CREATIVITY:** Developing one's artistic and imaginative abilities.

3) **EMOTIONAL INTELLIGENCE:** The ability to identify and manage emotions and appropriately engage with others.

4) **SPIRITUAL GROWTH:** Expanding one's knowledge and understanding of your personal value and belief system or philosophy and increase your ability to love and accept others.

5) **INTELLECTUAL DEVELOPMENT:** Continuously learning and developing new skills and knowledge.

You might ask, "Oh yes! I would love to do all of these, but how will I find the time to do it?" You find space for a few that can be accomplished. Don't pick everything at once; use the *commit and shift* approach described in Chapter 7.

First, review where you have interest and *pick and stick* to a few by selecting 1 to 3 activities from each area. Once conquered, come back, and add a few more. Constantly growing through small achievements gives you a sense of accomplishment and excitement to move to your next level.

To get you going, here are suggested ideas in each of the five areas of personal development:

PHYSICAL HEALTH & WELLNESS

- **EAT WHOLE, NUTRIENT-DENSE FOODS:** Include plenty of lean protein, fruits, vegetables, whole grains, and healthy fats in your diet.

- **REDUCE PROCESSED FOODS AND ADDED SUGARS:** Reduce processed foods: avoid packaged foods high in sugar, salt, and unhealthy fats.

- **DRINK MORE WATER:** Staying hydrated is essential for overall health, so drink plenty of water throughout the day.

- **INCREASE PHYSICAL ACTIVITY:** Find ways to be more active throughout the day, such as taking the stairs instead of the elevator, parking farther away from your destination, or taking a walk during your lunch break.

- **INCORPORATE STRENGTH TRAINING:** Building muscle can help increase metabolism and improve overall function.

- **GET ENOUGH SLEEP:** Aim for seven to nine hours per night to support healthy metabolism and energy levels.

- **REDUCE STRESS:** Engage in stress-reducing activities such as meditation, yoga, or deep breathing exercises.

- **SEEK GUIDANCE FROM A REGISTERED DIETITIAN OR PERSONAL TRAINER:** A professional can provide personalized recommendations based on your goals and lifestyle.

CREATIVITY

- **PRACTICE MINDFULNESS:** Being aware and present at the moment can enhance your creativity and help you generate innovative ideas.

- **CHANGE YOUR SURROUNDINGS:** A change in your environment will change your thought process and help you think creatively. Switching up your surroundings or workspace can improve your creativity.

- **TRY NEW THINGS:** Trying something new expands your scope of knowledge and can trigger new ideas.

- **TAKE BREAKS:** Allowing time to rest and step away from a project can help recharge your creativity.

- **COLLABORATE WITH OTHERS:** Working collaboratively can lead to innovative ideas that are impossible on your own.

- **EXPOSE YOURSELF TO DIFFERENT ART FORMS:** Watching films, reading books, or listening to music or podcasts can stretch your imagination in new ways.

- **TAKE A MUSIC OR ART CLASS:** Learning new art forms has numerous benefits, including cognitive, emotional, and mental wellness.

- **KEEP A JOURNAL:** Writing down your thoughts helps you process issues and ideas and provides additional inspiration.

EMOTIONAL INTELLIGENCE

- **PRACTICE SELF-AWARENESS:** Pay attention to your emotions, triggers, and responses in different situations. Recognize how they affect your behavior and decision-making.

- **DEVELOP EMPATHY:** Try to put yourself in others' shoes and see situations from their perspectives. Understand their emotions and reactions.

- **IMPROVE COMMUNICATION SKILLS:** Learn to express your emotions effectively and listen actively to others' feelings and thoughts.

- **MANAGE STRESS:** Develop healthy coping mechanisms for stress and anxiety, such as exercise or meditation.

- **SEEK FEEDBACK:** Ask for feedback from others on how you can improve your emotional intelligence and implement their suggestions.

- **DEVELOP EMOTIONAL REGULATION:** Learn how to manage your emotions and reactions rather than letting them control you.

- **LEARN CONFLICT RESOLUTION:** Resolve conflicts by practicing empathy and effective communication instead of escalating the situation.

- **INCREASE KNOWLEDGE:** Read books that discuss emotional intelligence and practice the principles discussed there.

SPIRITUAL GROWTH

- **MEDITATION AND PRAYER:** Pausing to reflect helps calm the mind and create inner peace, leading to a deeper connection with oneself and a higher power.

- **STUDY SPIRITUAL TEXTS:** Reading and studying spiritual texts can help you gain a deeper understanding of spiritual principles and guide you to live a more spiritually fulfilling life.

- **PRACTICE MINDFULNESS:** Being present at the moment and truly living in the present can help you feel more connected to your spirituality.

- **ENGAGE IN ACTS OF KINDNESS AND SERVICE:** Helping others can provide a sense of purpose and can help you feel more connected to the world around them.

- **CONNECT WITH LIKE-MINDED INDIVIDUALS:** Joining a spiritual community can provide a supportive and uplifting environment to help you grow spiritually. Be mindful of toxic religious mindsets that may instill fear or use judgment as a form of spiritual validity testing. Utilize practices and ideas that are elevating, not diminishing of you or others.

- **REFLECT ON PAST EXPERIENCES:** Reflecting on past experiences and examining how they have shaped your beliefs and values can help you better understand yourself and your spirituality.

+ **PRACTICE GRATITUDE:** Expressing gratitude for the people and experiences in your life can help create a more positive and spiritually fulfilling outlook.

INTELLECTUAL DEVELOPMENT

+ **READ WIDELY:** Reading a variety of books, articles, and other resources helps you expand your knowledge and understanding of different subjects.

+ **ENGAGE IN INTELLECTUAL DISCUSSIONS:** Having meaningful conversations with people who have different perspectives can challenge your thinking and help you see things from different angles.

+ **LEARN A NEW SKILL:** Learning something new will require you to activate new parts of your brain, helping develop new thinking pathways.

+ **TRAVEL AND EXPLORE:** Travel exposes you to new cultures, ideas, and ways of thinking. It can broaden your horizons and help you see things in a new light.

+ **TAKE ON CHALLENGES:** Challenging yourself pushes you out of your comfort zone and helps you develop new skills and abilities.

+ **ENGAGE IN CRITICAL THINKING:** Analyzing situations, asking questions, and evaluating evidence can develop your critical thinking and reasoning skills.

+ **ATTEND LECTURES AND WORKSHOPS:** Attending talks and workshops on different topics can help you learn new things and expose you to new perspectives.

+ **WRITE:** Writing is a fantastic way to clarify your thoughts and improve your ability to communicate your ideas.

+ **STAY CURIOUS:** Curiosity is the key to intellectual growth. Always ask questions and seek answers.

+ **PRACTICE MINDFULNESS:** Mindfulness practices help you develop focus, concentration, and awareness, which can help you grow intellectually.

TUNING IN AND CREATING PERSONAL SPACE

Now that you have a few ideas floating around, pause and tune into your personal development. This is your time to center yourself and find the time to invest in yourself! Using your checklist from each area, prioritize them and consider how you will create space.

Do you find time for creativity? Writing, reading novels, art, music, dance, or attending plays?

Do you feel physically well? Do you need more energy? Do you get enough sleep? Could you improve your diet or exercise routines?

Do you feel emotionally well? What are your emotional responses like? Do you handle stress well? Are there ways you could increase your emotional intelligence or emotional quotient (EQ)?

Are you increasing your knowledge and skills? What areas are you seeking to develop, and are you finding time to read and learn?

CHAPTER 21

Establishing Your Space

"Your personal space is your sacred space. Protect it, cherish it, and fill it with positive energy."

—TRINA CELESTE

I hear your thoughts, "I would love to do things for myself, but I just don't have the time!"

My question is, why not?

What are you prioritizing that makes you have zero time to go for a walk, play music, meditate, draw, read that book that is gathering dust on your shelf, or text someone who may need a positive boost? You are in control of your time, and you get to decide how you will create space. Intentionally creating time and space for self-reflection and self-care practices cultivates inner harmony.

I have caught myself in annoying time-suck riptides like *Candy Crush*. They should call the game "Time Crush," the ultimate time and space destroyer. The game began to consume all my free moments, and I forced myself to delete the app before my life was completely crushed.

Remember the goats? A goat may be one of the tangent trifectas of social media: TikTok, Facebook, or Instagram. It may be a game, streaming too much tv, home busyness, office house-work, or anything that takes priority over your personal development. The goats of distraction are the consumers of your personal space, and if you don't have time for yourself, then more likely than not, you are giving it to someone or something else less valuable.

I understand you can't, and shouldn't, be productive 100% of the time; we each require personal downtime. Consider making it a game and challenge yourself to slowly *shift time from consuming activities to blooming activities.* Before you know it, you may realize you no longer need that activity in your life.

Creativity, ideation, and burgeoning life designs quickly disintegrate in the tidal force of unnecessary distractions. These life-consuming goats attempt to minimize your efforts and push you to develop poor habits, eroding time and space and leaving you with nothing left for yourself. Neglecting your personal development puts both your mental and physical well-being at stake. Without sowing your seeds of knowledge, your potential to nurture a better world remains unattainable.

To combat the risk of undeveloped ideas and impact, review areas where you want to prioritize, plant, and grow, then reinforce your fences. You will see there are many opportunities for personal development in each area. Relationships, finances, work, and personal growth are intricately interwoven. Taking time for yourself ensures that every other area grows in tandem.

FINDING YOUR ROOM

Recently, I took my car to be serviced and had a few hours wait. In proper form, I thought I'd use this time to sit and work on the edits for this book. The room was spacious and empty other than one other gentleman, and I positioned myself across the room, opened my laptop, and got to work.

Moments later, a woman in a bright red floral shirt enters the room, charging directly to me, and plops down in the chair next to me. I looked around the room, seeing the seventeen other chairs available, and wondered what was so attractive in the seat six inches from me.

She pulls out her phone and starts a very loud yet not very profound conversation. I cannot focus, although I try. I put in my headphones, and it was no use. Her voice reverberated throughout the room. I made inquiring eye contact with the only other person in the room to see if he had also noticed the disturbance, which he had. He shrugged, rolled his eyes, and returned to reading his paper.

I thought she would end this conversation quickly. But no, as the minutes increased, I learned of each item on her exceptionally long grocery list, the fence she needed to mend, her frustrations with her daughter-in-law, and the extensive but not so exciting party plans for the coming weekend. I am not sure who was on the other end of the line, but I don't think they would have had time to say anything other than a mumbled, "Yeah, uh huh...uh huh" here and there.

I looked desperately around and saw that the mother's room tucked in the back corner was open. I packed my bags and carried them to the solaced space, which allowed me to focus. It was a serene heaven on earth, and I got into a deep flow that I didn't see the text informing me that my car had been finished two hours prior!

I reflected on how we each need to find room in our lives, whether it is your "Mother's Room," a "Father's Room," or a "Get Me the Hell Away from Everyone Room." Somewhere you can escort yourself into your "Isolation Oasis," basking in the glory of blissful solitude, far away from any maddening crowd.

Creating time and space for personal development does require intentional planning and commitment. Here are some steps you can take to make it happen:

REVIEW YOUR GOALS: Create and review your personal development goals frequently. What areas of your life do you want to improve? What skills do you wish to learn? What do you want to achieve in the long term?

SCHEDULE TIME FOR PERSONAL DEVELOPMENT: Once you have identified your goals, schedule time for personal development in your calendar. Make it a priority and treat it like any other important commitment.

CREATE A DEDICATED SPACE: Set up a dedicated space where you can focus on your personal development. This could be a quiet corner in your home, a coffee shop, or a library. Make sure this space is free from distractions and conducive to learning.

ELIMINATE DISTRACTIONS: Eliminate any distractions that may prevent you from focusing on your personal development. This may include turning off your phone or email notifications, closing your door, or using noise-canceling headphones.

MAKE IT A HABIT: Consistency is key to personal development. Make it a habit by committing to regular practice and progress toward your goals. This could mean setting aside a specific time each week or incorporating personal development into your daily routine.

Remember, personal development is a lifelong journey, so be patient and persistent in your efforts. Start with small achievable goals and increase over time. With time and dedication, you will create the time and space necessary to orchestrate life-work harmony.

FINDING TIME FOR PERSONAL DEVELOPMENT

Time to look over your priorities and the areas you have identified and want to develop. In this next section, we pull it all together. In each area of the four areas, what are the top priorities where you want to develop personally?

RELATIONSHIPS

Which skills would you like to develop to become a better spouse, partner, co-worker, friend, sibling, or parent? Below are some ideas of where you can build your relationships. Although uncomfortable, asking for feedback from others is a fantastic opportunity to expedite harmony at work and at home.

Feel free to stick to something other than this list. Center yourself on your version of harmony. What are your thoughts, and where you see there is an opportunity to grow?

- ☐ **COMMUNICATION:** Expressing your thoughts, feelings, and ideas clearly and effectively is crucial in building any relationship.

- ☐ **EMPATHY:** Being able to understand and respond to the emotions of others can help to create a deeper level of intimacy and trust.

- ☐ **ACTIVE LISTENING:** Being fully present and actively listening to the person you are interacting with can help to establish a deeper connection.

- ☐ **CONFLICT RESOLUTION:** Being able to identify and resolve conflicts respectfully and constructively can help to strengthen relationships.

- ☐ **FLEXIBILITY:** Being adaptable and willing to compromise can help to avoid conflicts and make the relationship more harmonious.

- ☐ **RESPECT:** Treating others with respect and kindness can foster trust and create a positive dynamic in the relationship.

- ☐ **SELF-AWARENESS:** Understanding your emotions, needs, and values can help you communicate more effectively and make better relationship decisions.

Checkmark 1 or 2 that you would like to work on. Select a day, time, and focus duration each week where you will dedicate time to learning and developing new relationship skills.

Day(s)	Time(s)	Durations(s)

FINANCIAL WELLNESS

Which skills can you develop to improve your financial education, preparation, and planning? Are there specific financial aspects you avoid? Do you need to set aside time to build habits in planning? Here are some suggested strategies for improving your fiscal management skills.

- ☐ **CREATE A BUDGET:** This will help you plan your income and expenses and identify areas to cut spending.

- ☐ **PAY OFF DEBT:** Start by prioritizing your high-interest debt and creating a plan to pay it off.

- ☐ **SAVE FOR EMERGENCIES:** Aim to save at least three to six months' living expenses in an emergency fund.

- ☐ **INCREASE RETIREMENT SAVINGS:** Consider contributing more to your retirement accounts or opening a new account if you do not already have one.

- ☐ **REVIEW YOUR INSURANCE:** Ensure you have adequate insurance coverage, including health, disability, and life insurance.

- ☐ **INVEST:** Consider investing in stocks, bonds, or mutual funds to increase your wealth over the long run.

- ☐ **STAY EDUCATED:** Read financial resources and keep up to date with financial news so that you can make informed financial decisions.

- ☐ **PLAN YOUR GOALS:** Set short-term and long-term financial goals and create action plans to achieve them.

Checkmark 1 or 2 areas where you see the most opportunity to improve your financial situation. Select a day, time, and focus duration each week where you will dedicate time to learning, planning, and engaging in economic development.

Day(s)	Time(s)	Durations(s)

WORK AND/OR COMMUNITY ENGAGEMENT

Which skills are you planning to increase as you develop your career? If you are not focused on a career now, how will you use your time for community engagement? What skills could you build to increase your effectiveness?

If you need a clear skills development plan, review the areas below and identify how you will create an actionable plan to develop your knowledge and employable skills.

- ☐ **IDENTIFY YOUR INTERESTS AND PASSIONS:** Think about what you enjoy and what makes you happy. This can help you identify the skills and education you need to pursue a career in that field.

- ☐ **RESEARCH THE JOB MARKET:** Look at the market trends and research which skills and education are in demand. This can give you an idea of what skills you should acquire for a competitive edge.

- ☐ **EVALUATE YOUR CURRENT SKILLS:** Assess your existing skills and determine which ones you need to improve or acquire to reach your desired career.

- ☐ **TALK TO PROFESSIONALS IN THE FIELD:** Speak to professionals working in roles you are interested in and ask for advice on the skills and education necessary to build a career.

- ☐ **CONSIDER CERTIFICATIONS OR COURSES:** Research degrees, certification programs, online courses, or college classes that can help you acquire the required skills and knowledge for your desired career or enhance your community involvement.

Checkmark 1 or 2 areas where you see the most opportunity to improve your work and/or community engagement. If not listed, write additional areas below and select days, times, and durations of focus each week where you will dedicate time to learning, planning, and engaging in work and/or community engagement.

Day(s)	Time(s)	Durations(s)

PERSONAL DEVELOPMENT

As you went through the previous chapter on creating space for yourself, which areas did you identify needing more time and space to increase your well-being? Do you need to allocate time for alone time, meditation, creativity, fitness, diet, or hobbies? Which areas of personal improvement would increase harmony in your life?

Identify 1 to 3 areas where you would like more space for yourself. Allocate space for yourself by selecting days, times, and durations of focus each week to which you will dedicate time for each activity.

Personal Action		
Day(s)	Time(s)	Durations(s)

Personal Action		
Day(s)	Time(s)	Durations(s)

Personal Action		
Day(s)	Time(s)	Durations(s)

LIFE-WORK HARMONY PRIORITY LIST

Congratulations! You now have a Life-Work Harmony priority list! You have created a "life first" approach to create space for yourself and your personal development in each area. To continue to build the habit of creating space for yourself, revisit this plan weekly.

Set aside time when you will look at and adjust your plan. Sundays are often a perfect day to plan for your upcoming week. Review your schedule and identify adjustments, and determine what you need to say *no*, or *not now* to. *How much easier will it be to say no, now that you know what you will say yes to?*

You are no longer balancing it all. You are no longer taking direction from anyone else but yourself. You are in the center of your life's garden, identifying what is most important and what is not. You can reinforce your fence lines and control the gates of who is allowed in and who is not.

That does not mean there will not still be challenges in finding sufficient time for everything you would like to do. Taking a few moments each day to tune in to see if your schedule requires adjustment helps you keep harmony throughout your day. To assist in this challenge, here are a few suggestions to help you stay on target.

UTILIZING TWO-FORS

Allocating two-for-one time is what I call a "Two-For." A two-for is when you merge and accomplish multiple goals simultaneously to use your time effectively.

Physical fitness is a priority for me every day. This is the one area in my life I rarely push to the side, and I will find time to get to some form of activity every day. However, finding time with friends has been a challenge as I committed to scaling a non-profit, a business, a family, and authoring a book. My best friend and I often plan our time together at the gym to ensure we still have time for our friendship.

There are myriad ways to enjoy a *Two-For*! Our students organize study buddy groups, providing opportunities to socialize, network, and develop skills together outside of the home. Some bring their kids to networking events, fostering a deeper understanding of career prospects while spending quality time together. Whether it's yoga sessions or financial investment groups with colleagues, these activities offer friendship, professional growth, and a chance to learn and support one another. And hey, if you incorporate food and drinks into the equation, you might even get some personal downtime!

While engaging in cardio warmups at the gym, I take the opportunity to review my schedule, eliminating or rescheduling any unnecessary appointments. I tackle my social media updates during leisurely walks in my post-workout wind-down. In the evenings, I enjoy preparing dinner while immersing myself in a captivating podcast. By seeking out these synergies with others, we nurture our personal growth, cultivate stronger relationships and contribute to the flourishing of those around us.

THE 20-MINUTE REWARD SYSTEM

To combat the fatigue of personal focus, I recommend implementing a personalized reward system. I call it the "20-minute reward" system. I structure my activities in increments of twenty minutes, and once I complete a productive task, I indulge in a rewarding activity. For instance, if I dedicate twenty minutes to weekly financial planning, I allow myself a leisurely walk or indulge in reading my favorite novel for twenty minutes. Similarly, if I spend twenty minutes at the gym, I grant myself twenty minutes of enjoyable Netflix time.

While the duration doesn't have to be precisely twenty minutes, it is a motivating timeframe to initiate an activity. Thirty minutes feels too lengthy, while ten minutes prevents substantial progress. Once I begin and I typically surpass the twenty-minute mark and exceed my initial time expectations.

You have various ways to reward yourself, and I'm confident you can find the right motivation that resonates with you. However, be mindful not to choose rewards that undermine achievements. For instance, twenty minutes at the gym doesn't equate to twenty minutes of eating ice cream! Apply common sense and select rewards that empower you and align with your life vision.

ACT OR BE ACTED UPON

Harmony is born from intentional action. Without purposeful activity, disharmony is likely to prevail. Stephen R. Covey's *7 Habits of Highly Effective People*, "Act or be acted upon," encapsulates the significance of defining your actions.[25] Merely going with the flow upon waking can lead to chaos, exposing us to others dictating our decisions. This puts us at risk of deviating from our envisioned growth and failing to accomplish what we desire.

However, it is crucial to avoid burning ourselves out. By clarifying what we will do and how and when we will do it, we can orchestrate an ongoing personal development journey. Stay grounded in your purpose and consistently remind yourself why you engage in each activity. Take moments to align with your commitments and prioritize self-space by reinforcing your well-being.

REINFORCING FENCES FOR PERSONAL SPACE

As a summary, I've included below a reminder of how to reinforce space for personal development. As a suggestion, copy and post somewhere to remember these reaffirming actions.

---

25   Covey, S. R. (1989). *The 7 Habits of Highly Effective People: Powerful Lessons in Personal Change*. Simon & Schuster.

1) **SET YOUR FENCE LINES:** Define your personal space. It is essential to begin by understanding what personal space means to you. This may include physical boundaries, emotional boundaries, and time boundaries.

2) **REINFORCE THE FENCE LINES:** Take the time to establish clear boundaries around your personal space. This may involve limiting your time with others or creating physical boundaries around your work or living space.

3) **KEEP OUT THE GOATS BY COMMUNICATING YOUR NEEDS:** Once you have identified your personal space needs, share them with the people around you. Let your friends, family, and colleagues know where you need space and privacy to feel comfortable.

4) **TEND TO YOUR MENTAL SOIL BY TAKING TIME FOR YOUR-SELF:** Give yourself enough time alone to recharge and refocus. You could spend this time doing activities that bring you joy and relaxation, such as reading a book, meditating, or practicing a hobby.

5) **COMMIT TO YOUR VISION AND PRACTICE SAYING NO:** Saying no is integral to creating personal space. It is important to be realistic about what you can take on and prioritize your needs without feeling guilty.

6) **PROTECT YOUR SPACE BY PRACTICING SELF-CARE:** Self-care is essential to creating personal space. This includes taking care of your physical health, getting enough sleep, and doing things that bring you joy and relaxation.

TUNE IN TO TIME AND SPACE

To get the benefits of Two-For, what activities can you merge time? How do you reward yourself for accomplishing goals?

What activities can allocate a small amount of time to do daily?

How will you reinforce your fences? Where do your personal fences need mending?

DOWNLOAD WORKSHEETS AND CONNECT
TO THE LIFE-WORK HARMONY FORUM AT
TRINACELESTE.COM

CHAPTER 22

Confronting the Invasive Pests of Sexism

"Stop working on growing a thicker skin and instead develop a stronger voice."

–TRINA CELESTE

For women, especially those of color, learning to identify and respond to intolerant and biased remarks is part of life's orchestration. Sometimes the remarks come at you as a bite here and a sting there, but they can add up over time, leading to more than mere annoyance and irritation. Dealing with constant comments of sexism or racist microaggressions has a negative impact on a person's mental and emotional well-being. Repeated exposure to such statements leads to frustration, anger, sadness, and helplessness. Their multiplied effect results in decreased self-esteem, increased anxiety and stress, and even physical health problems.

When comments are not stopped or left unaddressed, they lead to toxic work or social environments. They will leave you feeling marginalized, excluded, or discriminated against, affecting your performance and productivity, and ability to form meaningful relationships with colleagues and peers.

Tiny pests, seen and unseen, create rashes of responding rage and, if not addressed, lead to emotional unwellness. Harmony is challenging for those of us who deal with constant pest invasions, and sometimes we think we need to "shut up and put up" so we don't lose our jobs.

Sexism is real. Racism is real. Implicitly or explicitly, they both exist and alter your experiences in orchestrating harmony. I understand that due to my white privilege, I have not had to battle the pests of racism or experience the harmful impacts on the health of my life. My opportunities and ability to grow are not minimized by the time and energy required in swatting away racist comments and the stinging threat of unconscious bias due to the color of my skin. I recognize that people handle varying levels of interwoven complexity, and for them, pest control takes time and energy that others may not have to address.

The impacts and response methods fill up volumes of books as society seeks to address each deep-rooted issue of racial and ethnic biases. I will not attempt to address the full scope here; however, you can increase your awareness and be intentional in helping end or reduce the perpetuation of this plague of pests in society. And for sure, commit to never letting anyone on your watch become a part of promulgating it.

This chapter focuses on women and the impact of sexism as we search for harmony in our lives. However, for our male readers, I would ask you to continue with a mindset of openness as you search for a deeper awareness of the challenges of various life experiences different from yours.

As we focus primarily on the impacts of sexism, my goal is that the response tactics introduced here have applicability in resolving a broader set of life's pestilences. Through our awareness, we can then act and create change. This would include, but not be limited to, sexist or racist remarks, ethnicity biases, ageism, sexual orientation, body shaming, or gender identity discrimination.

SEXISM IS REAL

Sexism is not some "made up" thing where women are victims and must learn to "deal with it." As I have authored this book, every story, thought, and experience I have shared thus far has been tinged with the impact of sexist pests invading my life. Thoughts and feelings would emerge from deep within my psyche as I wrote. I hadn't realized how much pain was buried within me due to sexism. The stories would pop into my consciousness individually, and I would wonder, "What am I supposed to do with this?"

I put each one onto paper as they arose and then set them safely aside, not ignoring but waiting for the correct time to address them. These dormant stories, re-exposed, resulted in this chapter, and I share only a few of the hundreds that had once again surfaced from my consciousness.

As I drafted the story of me running for homecoming queen, I was reminded of a high school teacher I would catch peering over my shoulder and down my shirt as he walked behind me in class. At the time, I didn't understand that his anger and the shortness of his responses as he spoke to me were based on gender bias. His friendliness was only shown to my male classmates, and his objectification of me and his dismissiveness of my thoughts and comments have never been forgotten.

No one told me I would be dealing with this form of anger and dismissiveness my entire life. His and others' similar actions led me to spend too much of my life thinking something was wrong with me. If this is your thinking at times, I am telling you, there is nothing wrong with you other than living in a world that is challenged to accept you as you are.

In college, I caught classmates watching porn during class as the professor taught us how to code. As we deciphered the lines of code, my classmate disassembled the woman on their screen. I recall their snickers as they looked at me with objectifying sneers that made my stomach turn.

My college experience included professors telling blonde jokes, and being the only woman in the room meant those jokes were targeted toward me. Group projects where all the men received A grades, and the women were given B's, taught me that I had to fight every step to prove my intelligence was on par with the men in the room. One redeeming feature of our educational system was that tests could not introduce bias. I graduated with a 4.0 and made the Dean's List, learning to avoid classes that required group projects.

At my first job after receiving my computer science degree, I was told, "You are a risky hire." I learned that this is a common biased statement when hiring women. I was as qualified as the others on my team, but I felt I should be happy with what I could get. As I moved into my career, it was a common challenge for many of my colleagues to look me directly in the eye. Clients questioning my abilities based on my looks were the norm. At times, I would bring a male colleague to client meetings, prepping them beforehand with the questions to be addressed to get full responses.

On my first day as a technical engineer in 1998, I was instructed to build my computer from the scrap pile in the corner. Being new to corporate life, I didn't know that this was not the norm. I could feel my new team peering over my shoulder as I dusted off and pieced together working components. As each new male member joined the team, the IT team would deliver nice new machines and set them up for them making sure all was working appropriately. As a result of these and many other experiences, I responded by growing a "thick skin."

I moved through and forward into my career, thinking resiliency meant keeping my head down and not saying anything. Throughout my career, I was told, "You are too crisp, too bossy, too aggressive." These pesty stings were part of every lost job interview and all too common in performance reviews. I was seen as "too" outspoken, and it was often inferred I "should" diminish my existence.

After one of these job interviews, the hiring lead provided me feedback that I was "too crisp." A rash of rage hit, and I said, "What would you rather I do, give them a hug and bake them cookies, or get the job done?" Instead, I found an alternate position and continued to navigate through the swarming, biting clouds of sexism.

Fifteen years later, while interviewing at another tech company, I ran into one of the original panel interviewers who had decided I was "too crisp." He said, "I have felt horrible about turning you down all those years ago. You were the right candidate, and I didn't stand up to the pressure from the (all-male) panel." I appreciated his openness; however, it was too little too late, and my career and financial wellness had been impacted.

I share with you these stories not as a victim, nor am I looking for empathy. I wish to portray that I had the opportunity to speak up in these situations. However, other than the baking cookies comment, I was timid, and the fear of losing my job permeated my thoughts.

I have not met a woman in my thirty-year career who could not fill their own chapter of stories on the biting sting of sexist comments along with their emotions, fears, and indignant responses. Every individual who has expressed their stories shares the emerging feelings resulting from the sharp sting of unacceptance while trying to navigate their life and career.

What I have taken from these experiences is the opportunity to help others become further informed. We each (and I mean everyone) can become more aware of identifying and responding to sexism. Males, females, and non-binary must start with awareness and overcome discomfort in acting. Once you are aware, you cannot go back, and each time you act, it becomes inherently easier to speak up as an advocate for change.

Your actions and utilizing your voice are the pest control for these disharmonic invaders. To effectively and safely use your voice, you must first identify the pests in their harmful forms of sexism, racism, and intolerance.

PEST IDENTIFICATION

You may wonder, "What exactly is a sexist pest and how can I control it?"

First, let us tackle how to identify pests. In human form, pests are any person or persons forming expressions implicitly or explicitly in which you are harmed. Meriam-Webster defines it, "In its broadest sense, a pest is a competitor to humanity." Emotional damage or opportunity losses are often not experienced immediately; it builds up and erodes over time. The personal results may lead to deteriorated physical and mental well-being. Direct attacking pests are like snakes, wasps, bed bugs, fleas, or ticks, which may bite or sting with stereotypical comments like, "You really should be home with your kids."

Some pests do not attack directly. Instead, they contaminate your surroundings like a housefly, which lands on and contaminates your food. Impacts occur through implicit and unconscious biases, typically unexpressed, like *you are a mother and won't be able to handle additional stress*. These may include being excluded from activities, not promoted into leadership positions, or not accepted into graduate school. These tacit forms of sexism burrow into homes, workplaces, educational systems, and broader societies and are termite-like destroyers of cultural foundations.

Other pests may be like cockroaches who scuttle across the floor at night, creating unsanitary conditions for others. These pests stay together in the dark, hiding out in daylight. Their actions prevent society from developing as they make toxic decisions from a position of power. It shows in divisive politics, exclusionary legislation, and obstructive policies and can even occur within your family. You know they exist because you see the daily impacts in wealth and power shifts between those who have and have not. Being able to pinpoint and control these pests takes concentrated effort. Creating cataclysmic change might require societal shifts through large-scale bug bombing and implementing long-term eradication plans.

It can be overwhelming as you consider the scope of sexism and it's impacts, so I will simplify where you can start.

Identify those causing direct injury within your life and reinforce your fences by relaying your feelings and the harm being caused to you. I would assume that most of those close to us are not intentional in their sexist comments and are unaware of the impact they are having. Setting clarity in a statement of why it is causing harm allows you to release the emotion and the person stating it to stop their (hopefully) unintentional insensitivity.

However, boundary fence lines can only sometimes keep these pesty invaders out. It requires learning how to identify and respond to moment-to-moment experiences. To do this, utilize the foundational work you put in place in this book, starting with your mental health and instilled confidence – these give you the strength to speak up in the moment.

DEVELOPING A STRONGER VOICE, NOT GROWING THICKER SKIN

I implore you to stop working on growing that "thicker skin" and instead develop a *stronger voice*. You cannot find harmony without understanding the various aspects of sexism, learning how to respond, and developing the courage to do so. You will deal with pests consuming all you plant in your garden, eating up your energy, and destroying your mental soil without verbal pest control.

While attending a gala, a friend introduced me to a venture capital founder, assuming he would be a supportive advocate for the work we were doing with Tech-Moms. As I walked up, I put my hand out to shake his hand. His eyes scanned me from head to foot and back up, never looking me in the eye. "Yeah, you are too bossy," he said, adjusting his thick, black-rimmed glasses. Then, he looked back at his phone, completely ignoring me.

My direct response was, "What? I am not too bossy!" I then started looking around, wondering if I had been punked, thinking to myself, *does he not realize who I am or what I do?* It all felt like a horrible joke.

I pulled myself out of the shock and asked, "Why would you say that?" He was now in full ignoring mode as if I did not exist. He began frantically typing on his phone responding to what must have been a highly crucial message, or more likely, suddenly realized how badly he had verbally exposed himself. Instead of apologizing, he ignored me.

My friend who introduced me was floored, jaw and eyes wide. He looked at me, at him, and back at me, unsure what to do. He shrugged his shoulders and said nothing. Fortunately, we turned and met an individual who was more gentlemanly and gracious.

Sexism happens. It will continue to happen. You cannot change everyone abruptly; however, you can change how you respond and start spraying pesticides by having a voice. Months later, I was invited to the same individual's office. He remembered nothing of our first encounter; at least, that is what he let on.

So much of what is occurring in these scenarios is so profoundly unconscious many do not recognize they are doing it. You can be *firm* in first letting them know they have just expressed a bias, and then be *gracious* by letting the emotion go and not internalizing the statement or ruminating on it other than acknowledging it and moving on.

GOATSH*T! ALERTS, THE WORDS "TOO" AND "SHOULD"

First, we need to understand the goatsh*t! bias alerts of the words, *too*, and *should*. Like the VC who called me too bossy, both terms are based on the deep-rooted bias of how individuals *expect* you to be. When you do not live up to those expectations, you are told, "You are too…" and "You should…." You are being compared to a version of what they have envisioned a woman should be and how they should act and behave.

Do not internalize these statements, and instead respond, "I hear a potential bias in your statement. Could you please explain to me why you said that?"

Responding to sexist statements is never easy, and responding takes practice. Often, you may react to the shock of a statement and immediately respond defensively. Be okay with that, you have potentially been under attack for a long time, and your fighting senses will go off. If possible, catch it and ask, "Why do you say that?" They may get flustered as they recognize they just verbally vomited their bias on you. *Let them be flustered.*

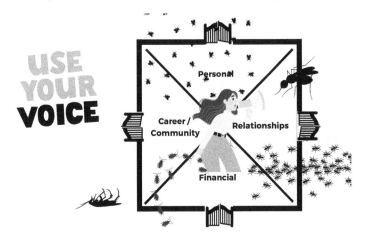

Develop a Stronger Voice

TUNE IN TO SEXISM

How is, or has sexism impacted your life's garden? Spend time reflecting on your experiences.

Has a manager ever made sexist comments or used their authority to make you feel small simply because you are a member of the opposite sex? Have they ever blocked your career, dismissed you, or threatened to fire you if you didn't do X, Y, or Z? How did you respond and why? Rewrite the scene with you using your voice to assert yourself and your needs.

Journaling and writing are remarkable ways to express your emotions, acknowledge them, think through your response, and then let the feeling go.

Find another person to share one of your experiences with. Write down how it feels to share these stories with others. Do you feel empowered?

JOIN THE LIFE-WORK HARMONY
FORUM AND SHARE YOUR STORIES AND
THOUGHTS ON RESPONDING TO SEXISM AT
TRINACELESTE.COM

CHAPTER 23

Speaking Up: Your Role in Pest Control

*"Sexism is a choice, once recognized demand change
through an intentional active voice."*

–TRINA CELESTE

The culminating stings of sexism will continue to wreak havoc and cause pain until you move from awareness to action and increase your confidence in stepping up and saying, "That is not okay." You are not helpless but are armed with a super-powered weapon— your voice. Do not underestimate the power of speaking up. This skill can be developed and needs to be charged up and activated.

When you do, it grounds and centers you in harmony with yourself, allowing you to feel empowered. It may not change the situation with an initial backlash, but in saying, "I was not okay with what you said," you give yourself power and peace.

Of all the women and men I have spoken with who have experienced the deep sting of a sexist comment in the workplace, each one has found it challenging to know how to respond appropriately. Typically, the correct response would come later after reflection. Even at 3 a.m., waking them from a dead sleep thinking, "Oh, if I had only said this!" *Finding the right thing to say is difficult; finding the courage to respond is even harder.*

How many times have you heard a sexist comment or situation which replays over and over it in your mind? It eats up your time, your energy, and your mental capacity. Being able to identify sexist or racist comments and learning to respond appropriately not only is a preventative measure from future pests within your life, but you are also reducing the potential for those same pests to infiltrate other gardens.

Develop your awareness of potential assaulting stings, then act to protect yourself. Within this chapter, I provide a high-level overview of the forms of sexism. Deeper dives into your experience and sharing stories along with their appropriate actions in a live form; whether with another individual, group training, online seminar, or forum is most beneficial.

For this reason, I created a Life-Work Harmony forum at trinaceleste.com where individuals can join and share their stories and evaluate potential responses. To ensure we do not become a venting and complaining platform, individuals pose questions and members provide proposed responses and support. The focus stays on the control action, not on the pest itself.

Pest control only occurs if the awareness is tied to actionable change. In discussions, you can reflect on the actions that need to be taken so you are armed and ready to respond when they happen.

As a high-level introduction, below are the forms of sexism which can infiltrate your life's garden, along with an initial suggested action to control:

1) **INSTITUTIONAL SEXISM:** Policies, practices, and traditions within organizations or institutions that perpetuate gender inequality.

   Control Action: Be aware of potential lack of promotions, lack of inclusion, limited feedback, or stretch assignments.

View policies or practices within your workplace that may be perpetuating inequality.

For example, when hiring recruits, we enacted a new policy requiring a woman to be on all hiring panels. As they engaged, one of the women on a hiring panel identified that the interviewers were asking different questions to the men than the women, not allowing them to provide a deeper understanding of their knowledge and skills. When reviewing all candidates, the panel stated that the women were not qualified. Enacting standardized questions and removing the possibility for bias through diverse panel interviews helped mitigate potential hiring bias.

2) **CULTURAL SEXISM:** Beliefs, values, and assumptions within a society that promote or enable gender inequality.

Control Action: Listen, watch, and hear how people speak about women. Reflect on what feels appropriate and what may be pushing sexist ideas into your family and community. When something feels wrong, you say, "That statement does not perpetuate healthy beliefs about women." Or "Help me understand why you said that?"

Chapter 4 delved into Alan's experiences as a presenting male in the workplace, and his position created unique situations to become a vocal ally. One day, during a lunch break, a friend shared a chat room created by a co-worker filled with sexist comments about women, mainly targeting their newly hired black female director. One remark stood out: "I refuse to take orders from a black woman. No woman is going to teach me how to sell."

Alan had developed relationships with many contributing to the chat and inquired with a close colleague to gauge his reaction. His friend responded, "I'm speechless. I don't have a problem with her." However, despite their disagreement, nobody spoke up. They silently scrolled through the hateful messages, absorbing them without taking any action.

Alan had his first meeting with the director a couple of days later. During their conversation, she genuinely asked him, "What drives you? What is your why?" She showed a sincere interest in his work and success. Encouraged by this connection, Alan mustered the courage to share his concerns with her. He ended the conversation by informing her of the inappropriate chats, saying, "I hate to bring this up, but for your safety and mine, I need to share." Acting upon his disclosure, the director promptly informed HR, leading to a two-day office shutdown for an investigation into the chat room. Eventually, the person responsible for creating the channel was identified and terminated.

However, the issues didn't end there. The fired individual began harassing employees on LinkedIn, leaving negative reviews on Glassdoor, and engaging in cyberbullying. It was not just a single step but a road of reinforcement in reporting and addressing ongoing harassment. Alan recognized that women and individuals of color face tremendous difficulty when speaking up. The fear of retaliation, personal attacks, isolation, and gaslighting is a real response, as evident in his experience.

Consequently, Alan was excluded from lunches and after-work drinks with the guys. Despite exclusionary responses, he continued to develop a strong voice and advocate for what was right. Consider what might have happened if he had never informed his director. The consequences would have been far more severe, leading to an even greater extent of harassment and toxicity within the workplace. Choose to speak up instead of attempting to fit in. Speaking up is typically not the popular route. However, it is the only route to making a significant positive impact.

You get to choose the impact you will leave on this world each time you decide to cower in the shadows of cultural toxicity or break the binds of bias in the workplace by using your voice. Speaking up is usually discomforting in the short run but results in harmony in the long run. Remember the big picture and broader impacts in mind to build courage in speaking your truth.

3) **INTIMATE PARTNER VIOLENCE:** Any physical or psychological harm of a sexual or non-sexual nature committed by a current or former partner.

Control Action: Emotional and financial abuse, and physical harm, must be stopped. The challenge is deepened with potential co-dependent situations or safety. If you are dealing with partner violence in any form, please seek help.

If you or someone you know is experiencing partner violence, there are several resources available for help:

- *Call emergency services:* If you or someone you know is in immediate danger, call 911 or your local emergency services.

- *Reach out to a hotline:* Many hotlines are available for domestic violence victims. These hotlines can provide immediate assistance and connect you with local resources. In the United States, you can call the National Domestic Violence Hotline at 1-800-799-SAFE (7233) or visit their website at thehotline.org.

- *Seek help from a shelter:* Domestic violence shelters provide safe accommodation to victims of partner violence. They can provide a safe place to stay, counseling, and other support services.

- *Talk to a therapist:* A therapist can provide emotional support and help you produce a plan to leave a violent relationship.

- *Contact a domestic violence organization:* Domestic violence organizations can provide legal assistance, counseling, and other services to victims of partner violence.

Partner violence is not your fault; you do not have to go through it alone. Many resources are available to help you stay safe and get your needed support.

Remember in the introductory chapter, the individual on the phone hiding and whispering? She is not the only woman I have met living in fear. The stories of control, abuse, and emotional and physical injury would fill volumes. It is a social undercurrent of pain rarely discussed and must be exposed. My encounters represent only a drip of the immense oceans of pain being endured without a voice.

The number of women currently suffering is more significant than it may appear. According to the Domestic Violence Hotline, an average of twenty-four people per minute are victims of rape, physical violence, or stalking by an intimate partner in the United States — more than 12 million women and men in a single year (about twice the population of Arizona).[26] If you are experiencing domestic violence, use the resources available to seek assistance, center on your life's vision, and take the necessary steps to allow harmony to flow into your life.

4) **HARASSMENT:** Unwanted or offensive behavior directed at someone in a way that creates a hostile or intimidating environment.

   CONTROL ACTION: You should report. Respond and report to authorities to ensure a safe environment, and you confirm that others are also safe. Do not dismiss or live in avoidance.

Harassment in the workplace should never be tolerated and should be addressed through appropriate channels. I had the privilege of mentoring Chelsea, a brilliant engineering graduate, who faced a distressing situation on her first day when a fellow employee made an inappropriate comment about what she was wearing. This began a series of escalating harassment incidents that she had to endure.

---

26 National Domestic Violence Hotline. (n.d.). Domestic Violence Statistics. Retrieved from https://www.thehotline.org/stakeholders/domestic-violence-statistics/

During a review, Chelsea's manager made inappropriate remarks about another female colleague, highlighting his refusal to hire her due to her attractiveness. She immediately responded, "That was completely inappropriate, and it is illegal not to hire someone based on their appearance." Chelsea courageously escalated the issue up two levels and requested the reassignment to a new manager.

Fortunately, the senior manager responded appropriately by involving HR and corporate compliance. While the process was challenging, Chelsea's Zula-like fierceness and bravery prevented the continuation of a toxic environment, and the company conducted a thorough investigation, took corrective action, and ensured a safer workplace for her.

Although the incident didn't eradicate inappropriate comments, Chelsea's experience empowered her to find her voice and engage with HR when faced with inappropriate comments or actions. Chelsea's ability to utilize her voice and report such incidents has become a crucial career skill, allowing her to maintain her power and create a safe working environment.

Chelsea expressed surprise at receiving appreciation from her female colleagues and male team members. Many male employees had been discomforted by the constant "locker room talk" from the manager, and Chelsea's actions had indirectly given them the courage to address the issue.

5) **GENDER-BASED DISCRIMINATION:** Unequal treatment of individuals based on their gender rather than their abilities or qualifications.

   CONTROL ACTION: Awareness is critical in this situation as it has subtle impacts on pay, promotion, or inclusion of women. If identified, ask probing questions as to why decisions are made.

For example, someone told me, "I don't hire women because they just go on maternity leave."

My response opened a discussion with multiple points, "Why would you say that? Do you offer parental leave? Do you think men might like to care for their children as much as women? Also, you do realize this is discriminatory and illegal?" Whether he decided to accept my responses or continue discriminatory action, I do not know. Still, at this moment, I could introduce the idea that *men are part of the parental equation.*

Sometimes, we can call out inappropriate actions; at other times, we can inform. It is up to you and what your emotional state requires. Stay centered, and do not allow conversations to consume you more than they should.

A typical response to gender discrimination and equality is, "Well, I believe in meritocracy." So do I, and I would love to see meritocracy and equality as the norm. However, in the biased culture which we are in, meritocracy does not exist. Without intentional work to remove or circumvent the deep-rooted biases, meritocracy will not occur.

6) **STEREOTYPING:** Making assumptions or generalizations about individuals based solely on their gender.

   CONTROL ACTION: Begin by listening for when stereotypes occur and then counter these with a curiosity approach. You may have a relationship where family members push stereotypes about a woman's role. Stand up and reinforce your identity by saying, "Your idea of who you think I should be is based on a stereotype that I do not accept."

While attending Harvard Business School, I was researching how to build compelling business culture strategies. As I discussed my work on women in leadership with my professor, she stated, "I deal with stereotypes often. When I come to class, students will ask me to copy a paper or get them coffee, assuming I am the student admin. I would respond, no, I am your professor." Sometimes a short, direct response creates all the necessary control required, resulting in a subtle shift in awareness of gender roles and stereotypes.

7) **SEXIST JOKES AND LANGUAGE:** Using derogatory or objectifying language or jokes based on gender.

CONTROL ACTION: You do not have to laugh or accept. Say, "That joke was not appropriate. Please do not use that remark in the future."

A common response to being shut down is anger. *Let them be angry; you do not have to respond to it.* Walk away, and as I have heard psychologists and my mom suggests, "Step to the left, and walk around it."

8) **OBJECTIFICATION:** The treatment of a person as an object, often emphasizing their physical appearance or sexual attributes at the expense of their individuality or humanity.

CONTROL ACTION: The challenge here is this can be indirect or direct. If a direct objectification occurs, you can say, "You are objectifying me/others; this is inappropriate." You can respond to immediate situations and increase awareness of subtle discomforts creating disharmony.

At a work-related golf tournament this year, I was assigned to join a random group of four players. An individual introduced himself to the others in the group, asking their name and then where they worked, sizing up their ability to expand their network. He turned to me and said, "And I see you are here as eye candy." Not asking my name or what I do, minimizing me as someone who is only there for their visual pleasure.

My response: "No, I am not here as your eye candy. My name is Trina, and I am an executive on the board for the golf tournament you are at." I did not say it with emotion but as a fact. You do not need to say anything further. At times you may feel like you need to educate someone, but you do not, stay short and direct with no need to explain.

I had a colleague that would come into the office and talk about all the women he saw at the gym, "There were so many fine specimens at the gym today." I stood up and said, "I wonder what your wife thinks about how you're speaking? Not appropriate."

His jaw dropped as his fists clenched and anger emerged, and I turned around and walked away. My fellow team members observed our interaction, and in a moment of awkward astonishment, they became educated that statements like this were unacceptable. Guaranteed, they second-guessed themselves the next time they wanted to express sexually objectifying statements at work.

9) **PAY INEQUALITY:** The difference in pay between genders, where women are often paid less than men for performing the same job.

   CONTROL ACTION: Become aware of your role's expectations in pay, understand how to negotiate salary, and once hired, ask your human resource team about pay scale ranges and promotion opportunities. You can regularly discuss career development with your manager and understand your goals and how you can scale your career and pay.

I was told twice in my career, "Trina, you didn't get that promotion because [the other candidate] has a family to be provided for." I did not understand at the time that this was discriminatory, or that I could say something. I did nothing then, and now do not want anyone else to sit quietly, not emboldened to respond. The consequences to your career, financial well-being, and personal self-worth are too detrimental.

This discrimination comes in the form of stereotyping, which infers that women are always the secondary income and do not need money as much as men. A student recently reported that this was said to her, and this form of sexism still exists. Be aware of pay inequity issues, know your value, and get comfortable asking pay-related questions.

YOU ARE THE POWER FOR CHANGE

As you explore the various facets of sexism, it's essential to pause and consider how each aspect might affect your life's harmony. No one is exempt from its impact. If you are a woman, you will inevitably encounter sexism. Your nieces, friends, aunts, mothers, and daughters will face sexism.

The fact that we fail to provide adequate training for our children on recognizing and responding to these issues perpetuates the problem. Ideally, education on this subject should be mandatory for teachers and professors, and it should commence from the earliest stages of a child's development.

Recognize your power in being able to create change. Now is the time to become aware, identify, and act. You can be the one who educates your sons and daughters on the fact that sexism exists, as well as how to identify it and begin the work to control this plague on society.

When my son, Skye, was fifteen, he came to me and said, "Mom, if you keep giving all the jobs to women, there won't be enough for the men." This was my son, who I had fed, educated, and raised as a single mom who knew I was the sole provider for my family. Yet, societal influences have created a scarcity mindset that there is not enough room for both men and women to work. It was a wonderful opportunity to discuss sexism, the importance of awareness of negative influences, and to be cautious in our thinking and actions.

This form of acting to create life harmony is not typically easy at the moment; however, as you act, it becomes easier for yourself and others in the future. When this same son became a senior in high school, I received a call from the principal's office. She informed me that my son had reported a male student who was texting nude pictures to female students at the school. My son recognized that the girls did not feel safe enough to report the unsolicited sexual abuse, and in this case, his awareness exposed criminal actions, and the police were involved.

At the risk of being ostracized by his friends, Skye felt empowered to act on behalf of female classmates stopped future women from being digitally attacked. The student was removed from school, and we hope that he received appropriate corrective care. With the disruption to behavior happening earlier rather than later in his life, it may have prevented an even more severe sexual assault from occurring.

To the men reading this chapter, you have a role in addressing sexism, not only in your awareness of your own biases but in speaking up when you hear it from others. It impacts you indirectly in creating disharmonious work environments and relationships. Your daughters, wives, sisters, and female friends will benefit from your ability to use your voice on someone's behalf. Whether you hear your friend tell someone they are "too bossy," objectifying someone at a golf tournament, or using locker room talk – please speak up and say, "Hey, that is not okay."

TUNING INTO YOUR ROLE IN PEST CONTROL

What if you woke up tomorrow and were the opposite gender? How would your life be different?

Thinking through your areas of influence, where and with whom could you create broader awareness? Where can you speak up, educate, and help eradicate sexism?

As you have read this chapter, what stories have bubbled up for you? Write them down and identify, without judgment, how you could have responded and acted. Was there a situation where you were proud of how you responded?

In reviewing all the forms of sexism, is there one that stands out? Which is it, and is there an action you can take today to control it?

CHAPTER 24

Conducting Your Life's Rhythm

"Within each of us is the power to create harmony with ourselves and with the world."

–TRINA CELESTE

The focus of this book has been on learning to put your life first to orchestrate harmony, and in doing so, you now bring others into harmony with you. Becoming a master of life-work harmony means we care for ourselves, but we tend to others as we become proficient at centering ourselves. This is not being self-centered. Becoming aware of our current mental health, our relationships, work, finances, and personal development allows us to understand when we need to tune in and tend to ourselves for a period, then once cared for, push outward, and tend to others. This is the orchestration of life.

I love watching band documentaries, including older bands like U2's "Rattle and Hum" or Pink Floyd's "Dark Side of the Moon." I derived my musical interest by watching my father, a singer, playing guitar in his country band called "Silver Sage." He would spend his free time learning new songs, always practicing, and playing at various chuckwagon dinners and social functions. I grew up listening to his deep baritone, Johnny Cash sound-alike voice daily. Old school country songs filled my home, and my brothers and sisters were accustomed to evenings filled with his renditions of Willie Nelson and The Oak Ridge Boys.

I would listen and watch him learn, practice, revise melodies, and work to harmonize with the band. I enjoyed watching the process and work of how musicians and bands formed and the struggles they experienced in learning to harmonize with each other while individually developing musical talents. Every musician's story has a time of angst, frustration, and even fury until they push through and find that harmonious buzz and success.

When harmony is achieved in your life, all areas come together in an arrangement that adds the feeling, depth, texture, and tranquility we all yearn for. What the greatest bands have found is how to understand other chords and combine them with their musical abilities in tandem to create innovative and emotionally moving music.

You orchestrate with others as your master your life harmony. This book's intent is not to become self-centered but to learn to center and then combine with others around you for an aligned purpose.

This combination of different pitches and chords is played or sung simultaneously to create a pleasing sound. Using a similar approach to finding harmony in music, seeking harmony is the same in life. Using the tips outlined in this chapter, you can gain insights and guide you through to mastery of life-work balance.

CONTROLLING YOUR LIFE'S RHYTHM

The rhythm of life can be so hard to keep pace with harmony. Life shifts the tempo as it gets disrupted and slows down with a focus on the sickness of a child or speeds up at the launch of a new project at work. Know that these tempo shifts will occur, and instead of reacting, respond in control of your rhythm rather than being carried away by it. A few suggestions:

1) **YOU SET THE TEMPO:** The tempo is the speed at which the music is played. You choose when in your life you want to place the accents. As the conductor and leader of your life, you select the beat by indicating the desired speed you want to go in everything from work to home life.

2) **USE ACCENTS AND DYNAMICS:** Accents are notes or beats emphasized in a piece of music. As we go through life, some situations require us to increase the speed and intensity of our actions.

3) **PAY ATTENTION TO TIMING:** Timing refers to placing notes and beats within the musical structure. As a conductor, you must be aware of the timing and ensure that all surrounding instruments are in sync in your symphony, communicating and coordinating timing with others.

4) **USE RESTS AND PAUSES:** Rests and pauses are silent spaces in the music. By using them strategically, musicians create a sense of anticipation or emphasis. In your life, resting and pausing provide you with a moment to recover, rejuvenate, and recenter. Critical "time outs" in your life's music will move you through the phases of your life with striking emphasis.

Imagine yourself singing your version of the lyrics below. Everyone will have a different tune, rhythm, and melody; every unique combination is right.

YOUR LIFE FIRST LYRICS

You don't have to be perfect, and you don't have to be right

Stay centered and listen, and you will find the light

Harmony will find you, it's perfect time pours

And leaves you dancing to the beat of a song that's yours

As you bring your song to life, intentionally enhance your tune by bringing others into harmony. Below are some shared secrets in harmonizing with others.

5 SECRETS FOR HARMONIZING WITH OTHERS

1. PRACTICE TOGETHER REGULARLY

Like a band that practices playing together, they learn how to create harmony with one another, practicing group harmony. This means getting comfortable with other's playing styles, understanding each other's strengths and weaknesses, and finding ways to complement each other.

2. LISTEN AND BE AWARE OF EACH OTHER

To create harmony, each group member needs to be able to hear what the others are playing. This means being attentive to other's parts and adjusting playing as needed.

Judgment has no place in a world of harmony. Instead, we must seek to understand one another. This happens as you listen with sincerity. Being aware and accepting of the importance of the parts others play in the world adds to a better and broader symphony.

3. EXPERIMENT AND IMPROVISE

There is no perfect way to do anything; altering methods allows for improved performance. Experimenting with chord progressions lets you see which will produce the best sound. Understand when something is not working and be open to collaborating on solutions.

4. NOT SINGING SOLO AND USING BACK UPS

You can bring in others with the right pitch or vocal ability to enhance harmonies. You will find it challenging to find harmony by singing all the parts yourself! Find where you can get a "backup singer" for help, delegate responsibilities, and free up valuable time and space for yourself.

5. GET FEEDBACK FROM OTHERS

Connect with others to provide advice on how and where you could improve and expedite your development. Don't expect to know everything. No one picks up and starts playing an instrument flawlessly without instruction. It is okay to rely on guidance from counselors, professionals, financial experts, fitness coaches, nutritionists, educators, music teachers... the list goes on. Help and guidance are available for anything you are challenged by or for enhancing areas where you want to grow.

TUNING INTO LIFE'S RHYTHM

How do you see you can harmonize with others in your life?

Are there moments when you feel you are controlling life's rhythm? When are these moments?

When do you feel you are at the wrong pace? How can you pause and reset the tempo in these moments?

CHAPTER 25

Living a Life in Harmony

*"Embrace the path of self-prioritization, put your
life first, and exemplify courageous living."*

–TRINA CELESTE

I sincerely hope a shift has happened as you have read these pages and taken the time to participate in each chapter's tuning-in moments. You have become aware of who you are and what is most important to you. You have set a vision, defined your purpose, set priorities, protected yourself, and centered yourself in your life garden.

I cannot overstate the importance of persistence in pursuing your version of life-work harmony. Remember, success is not a destination but a journey that requires ongoing effort in courageous living; setbacks and failures are an inevitable part of your journey. By staying committed to your goals and continuing to act towards achieving them, you will create a life that is both successful and fulfilling.

As you continue your journey, use the Life-Work Harmony model outlined in the remainder of this chapter to develop daily reflection habits. Any moment you feel disharmony, sit down and draw an X across a piece of paper and fill in the four areas: relationships, financial, career/community, and personal.

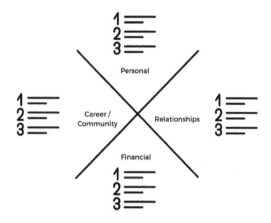

Prioritizing life-work harmony

List your priorities in each area for the day, week, or year. Is there anything on your schedule that does not align with your priorities?

Draw your fences; where should you set boundaries in each area? Are there areas you need to reinforce that will provide you with *light*, *air*, *water*, *nutrition*, and *space* to grow effectively?

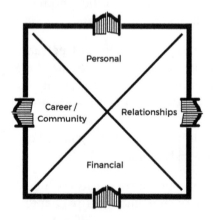

Controlling the gates

How are you doing mentally? Are there emotional challenges that need to be worked through? How can you get help? What behaviors may help in managing while you focus on your priorities?

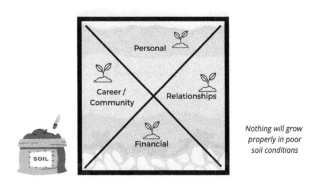

Fertilizing the soil of mental health

Are the weeds of fear, doubt, shame, or guilt overtaking your garden? What needs to be plucked and chucked? Is there anything you can flip or use to your benefit?

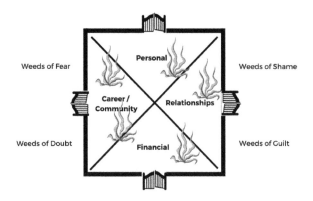

Pulling the weeds

Where are the goats? Have any crossed the fence lines and need to be returned to pasture?

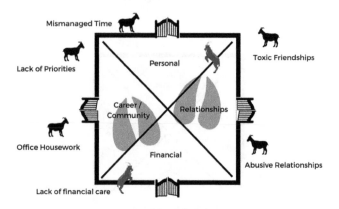

Goats that consume

Now you are ready to bloom! Remind yourself of your vision and priorities in each area. Where can you invite gardeners to help you bloom in any of the four areas?

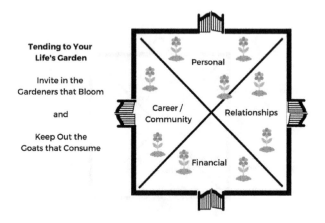

Tending to your life's garden

FINAL TUNE IN

Put you at the center of the garden

You have stopped trying to do it all and be it all. You have done the self-discovery work to find your vision and purpose with set personal goals. You are now equipped with the tools to implement harmonious actions daily. You have a newfound skillset in which you can fan the flame and build a broader knowledge and network to support you in your goals. You are now centered on your life first.

THE WOMAN IN THE ARENA

Hundreds of books, writings, and speeches have had deep meaning and impact throughout my life. One was Theodore Roosevelt's 1910 "Citizenship in a Republic" speech, also known as "The Man in the Arena." Consistent with my other writings, I have adjusted the gender reference, altering the meaning with an invitation for women to actively join in "the arena."

THE WOMAN IN THE ARENA

"It is not the critic who counts; not the woman who points out how the strong woman stumbles, or where the doer of deeds could have done them better.

The credit belongs to the woman who is actually in the arena,

whose face is marred by dust and sweat and blood; who strives valiantly;

who errs, who comes short again and again,

because there is no effort without error and shortcoming;

but who does actually strive to do the deeds;

who knows great enthusiasms, the great devotions; who spends herself in a worthy cause;

who at the best knows in the end the triumph of high achievement, and who at the worst, if she fails, at least fails while daring greatly;

so that her place shall never be with those cold and timid souls who neither know victory nor defeat."

You exist within the arena fighting unseen and unheard battles for far too long. You fight for your place in the world, often with pushback and judgment. You belong in the arena as a light at the center of the stage. Do not let fear, doubt, shame, or guilt stop you. I recognize your valiant efforts and ongoing determination. Do not give up or give in to those that do not understand your vision. Do not pay heed to those that would deter you from becoming who you are meant to be.

Remember, your strength comes from within, and as you put this work into determined action, you are a force for change like no other in the world. You are not alone in the arena; thousands are shifting to their rightful place at the center of the stage; they have placed themselves now as the conductor and raise their batons at the ready. Take a breath, center, tune in, and now—bring yourself forward in orchestrated life-work harmony.

Afterword

As I have shared stories of my life-work harmony journey, I have experienced fear, doubt, shame, and guilt. I've had to pluck, chuck, and flip these feelings thousands of times which were partnered with accompanying thoughts like:

"What if no one likes it?"

"What if I've wasted my time?"

But in the end, I pulled through and had to listen to my own advice: "It doesn't matter, write it anyway."

I set my fence lines firmly prioritizing my writing, asking myself continually, "What is most important?" My inner response always came back loud and clear: "Write your damn book." (Apologies for my potty mouth, this is just how I think at times.)

I have had to say no hundreds of times. I've had to stop and pause in my writing efforts and orchestrate life harmony, recognizing that I had to manage my time and that publishing this book was never a "no" but often a "not now."

I resisted urges to tidy up, organize a drawer, get on social media, start a new work project, or get caught up in office distractions. All my forced statements of no were required to stay focused on completion. I had to keep out the "goats" of others' requests, saying no to speaking engagements, networking events, friends' dinners, or handling a family member's issue.

I gave myself time to breathe and let the ideas flow. Incidentally, the idea for this "life-work harmony" model appeared on a break while cycling at the gym, as a flash in my mind resulted in a hurried sketch of the model scribbled at the back of the book I was reading.

I budgeted and allocated finances to make this book a reality, trusting my vision and remembering that I should invest in myself. I am grateful to my husband, who supported my vision as I temporarily lowered my client workload and income. I have deeply valued our conversations on why this work was a priority and respecting the importance of allocating time as we crafted a shared vision.

I relied on relationships and conversations with hundreds throughout the prior year on their insights into attempting to balance and seeking harmony -- too many to appropriately identify. Thank you to all those who willingly provided advice and guidance as I worked through every step of discovery in publishing. Having to start, stop, and restart three times with various editing teams was an act of determination, but I persevered with my eyes on my vision and a laser focus in completing this work.

Thank you to the team at GWN Publishing, Lil Barcaski, Kristina Conatser, Linda Hinkle, and Kristina Rodriguez for guiding this work through to becoming a reality. Forever grateful for your ability to take my big ideas and move them into reality and into readers' hands and minds. Zach Kristensen, thank you for staying engaged – even when not required. Laney Hawkes, thank you for your insights and perspectives, you pushed me to value my voice over others. A special thank you to Jenie Skoy for orchestrating my words to find their meaning and harmony.

My orchestral life-work harmony maneuvers became tantamount throughout the final months of completion as my father battled cancer. Many of these pages were written and edited in multiple hospitals and doctors' offices. At times we would sit in silence for hours, my typing only interrupted by nurses visiting with vitals, blood draws, and updates on progress. My time spent traveling and connecting with my father enhanced my stories, and prompted me to finish regardless with his reassuring, "You are doing more than you realize. Put yourself and your work first."

But most of all, what moved me forward was my purpose. I authored this book for the hundreds of Tech-Moms, and thousands of others open to hearing and acting on the message of life-first courage. Thank you for listening. I write for you as I have seen and know your struggles, pressured to carry the load from all sides, and challenged by the complexities of life and work. Your stories have been in my thoughts and mind as I've shared my journey. Together, we are sisters and brothers in arms, ready to bloom.

To continue your journey, I invite you to join the Life-Work Harmony forums at trinaceleste.com and connect with others sharing ideas and orchestrating their life-first harmony. Share your insights from this book with your organization, communities, families, friends, and colleagues. Together, in shared fierceness, we can be the force for change in our collective desire for life-work harmony.

About the Author

Prepare to be captivated by the extraordinary life journey of Trina Celeste—an embodiment of resilience, dedication, fierceness, fun, and unwavering passion. With over three decades of experience in the ever-evolving world of business and technology, Trina has risen as a distinguished figure, making a profound impact through her groundbreaking contributions for women in the workplace.

Trina's story takes you beyond the realm of tech, weaving a tapestry of personal triumph and fulfillment amidst the breathtaking foothills of Utah's majestic Wasatch mountains and through rural valley farms. She and her husband orchestrate a blended family of eight remarkable children, fostering an environment where love and support thrive.

Fueled by a profound commitment to empowering individuals and organizations, Trina has blossomed into a revered, award-winning culture and leadership consultant. Her unparalleled insights, cultivated through years of executive experience at some of Silicon Valley's largest companies, serve as a guiding light, inspiring others to achieve excellence and embrace personal growth.

Yet Trina's true passion extends far beyond her professional pursuits. She intimately understands the pressures women face today and recognizes that fostering harmony in the workforce is integral to preserving cherished family values. In a remarkable embodiment of her beliefs, Trina co-founded Tech-Moms. org, a non-profit organization on a mission to transform the lives of women through comprehensive career development. Through this noble endeavor, Trina empowers women, equipping them with the skills and opportunities to thrive, ensuring successful careers, and nurturing strong, resilient families.

Trina's awe-inspiring journey epitomizes a life dedicated to her purpose, integrity, and unwavering commitment to making a positive impact. Her story weaves together triumphs over adversity, the enduring power of love and family, and unparalleled professional excellence—her extraordinary twenty-five-year-in-progress vision of seeing more women successfully orchestrate life and work brought to fruition.

Immerse yourself in "Orchestrating Life-Work Harmony" and prepare to be uplifted, inspired, and forever transformed. Trina's wisdom and transformative experiences will leave an indelible impression upon your heart and soul, empowering you to pursue your dreams and orchestrate a life of harmony and fulfillment.

Printed in the USA
CPSIA information can be obtained
at www.ICGtesting.com
JSHW010956060823
46036JS00001B/1